LEAD YOUR LIFE

LEADERSHIP DECODED FOR COMMON MAN UNCOMMON & RESULTS

VINAY RAJ PARETA

Dedicated to

My Parents

My Teachers

My Mentors

My Friends

And above all,

My Guru!

Contents

Introduction *vii*

1. What Is Leadership? 1
2. Leadership In Action 8
3. Traits Of Great Leaders 23
4. Skillset For A Leader 43
5. Self Mastery 80

Epilogue 89

Introduction

Life has been kind to me that I've got some amazing mentors and friends in life. They've ensured that I not just learn to get up every time I fall, but also made sure I don't stumble at the first place!

Lead Your Life is based on whatever I've learnt and grasped from them along with the multitude of books I have read over the last decade. It shares with you how to evolve, stay relevant and ride the wave of change in the modern uncertain times.

This book is an attempt to turn you, my wonderful readers, into powerful leaders. This is neither a motivational book nor a research paper. It is a new-age guide that decodes the mystery around leadership and translates it into simple, clear and actionable concepts.

Hope it helps you unleash the leader in you.

CHAPTER ONE

WHAT IS LEADERSHIP?

> "*If your actions inspire others to dream more, learn more, do more and become more, then you are a leader. - John Quincy Adams*"

Leadership is the ability to inspire a team to achieve a certain goal. Though it is usually discussed in the context of business, leadership is also how you, as an individual, choose to lead your life.

The actual definition of leadership is to influence, inspire and help others become their best selves, building their skills and achieving their goals along the way. You don't have to be a CEO, manager or even a team-lead to be a leader.

Whether you're a CEO of a Fortune 500 company or a college student attempting to manage a pile of homework, leadership is about creating and sustaining lasting positive changes in your life and the lives of people around you.

So we can conclude that, "*Leadership is a skill and a tool you can gradually develop and use to create an impactful change.*"

This world needs human beings behaving like leaders more than ever before, mindful of the fact that they will leave a legacy. It is up to you whether it will be a positive one or not.

Never underestimate your ability to be a leader even if it means being a good dad, a good mom, a good sibling, a good friend or even a good grandparent. It is about the impact that you have on a single person, however small it is.

If you look at the world today, we have been facing unprecedented challenges like terrorism, global warming, soil erosion, environmental issues and mental health issues. Such issues were never faced by our ancestors at the current scale and magnitude. When we are faced with such unique challenges, we also need some extraordinary leadership.

Busting the myths around Leadership

Who comes to mind when you think of a successful, intelligent and talented person? Perhaps someone like the great inventor Thomas Edison, whose invention of light bulb has made it a symbol for moments of brilliance!

But, while Edison was a highly intelligent and talented individual, he wasn't born as a success. And he didn't develop the light bulb in one day, or even on his own. It took a long, slow process of curiosity, dedication and hard work.

Now let us first bust the myths around what leadership is and what it is not. This will help us establish in our minds that we are all equally capable to lead.

- *Myth:* Leaders are born with some innate magical quality that allows them to lead better than others.
- *Fact:* Leadership is a set of skills you can learn.

- *Myth:* Leaders are not afraid of anything.
- *Fact:* Leaders don't let their fears control them.

- *Myth:* Great leaders always take the right decisions.
- *Fact:* Leaders do make mistakes but they learn a lesson from it and move on.

- *Myth:* Leadership is a position or title.
- *Fact:* Leadership is an attitude.

- *Myth:* Leaders have charismatic personalities.
- *Fact:* Not necessarily. Those with charisma don't automatically lead.

Start with "Why"

In his phenomenal work *Start With Why,* Simon Sinek talks about why it is important to find your why in life. The same needs to be done by aspiring leaders as well. Discover your WHY – your purpose, passion and vision. This is foundational to anything in life, including leadership.

Work on mindset

Renowned Stanford psychologist Carol Dweck in her book, *Mindset* says that it's not intelligence, talent or education that sets successful people apart. It is their mindset, or the way that they approach life's challenges.

Let us explore a little more on Dweck's idea of mindset, how a "fixed mindset" can hold you back and how a "growth mindset" can help you to reach your goals.

According to Dweck, people either have a fixed or a growth mindset and the one that you adopt can affect every aspect of your life.

A *fixed mindset* is the belief that your intelligence, talents and other abilities are set in stone. You believe that you're born with a particular set of skills and that you can't change them.

If you have a fixed mindset, you will likely fear that you may not be smart or talented enough to achieve your goals. You may even hold yourself back by engaging only in activities that you know you can do well.

Worse still, a manager with a fixed mindset may fear that his team members' achievements will surpass his own. Or he may feel threatened if someone else spots an opportunity that he missed. He may even discourage a star team member's development and ignore their people's needs.

Dweck and her colleagues examined the brains of people with different mindsets. The brains of those with a fixed mindset showed higher activity when they were told that their answers to a series of questions were right or wrong – they were keenly interested to know whether they had succeeded or failed. But they showed no interest when researchers offered them help to learn from their mistakes. They didn't believe they could improve so they didn't try.

If you have a *growth mindset*, you believe that with effort, perseverance and drive, you can develop your natural qualities.

Whether your personality is determined by nature or nurture is still heavily debated, but according to Dweck, you can develop your own skills, abilities, talents and even intelligence through your experiences, training and effort.

You use feedback and mistakes as opportunities to improve, while enjoying the process of learning and becoming more productive. This is what Dweck calls *purposeful engagement*.

You also believe that you can overcome obstacles. You choose to learn from the experience, work harder and try again until you reach your goals.

In her research, Dweck built on the theory of neuroplasticity, which is the brain's ability to continue to form new connections into adulthood, after it has been damaged or when it is stimulated by new experiences. This supports the idea that you can adopt a growth mindset at any time of life.

You may not become another Thomas Edison but a growth mindset can help you to realise your own potential through learning and practice.

This is why Dweck says that offering praise when someone does well reinforces a fixed mindset while praising their effort encourages growth. When you focus on an individual's results, they learn that trying doesn't matter. But praising their efforts rewards their process of learning, so they become more motivated to keep striving toward their goals.

Though Carol Dweck advices to praise effort more than results, she also warns that to be truly praiseworthy, effort must be effective.

And she emphasizes that a growth mindset goes further than being positive and open-minded. It also requires focused effort in the right direction.

Pro Tip: You can begin working toward your goals by writing your own *Personal Mission Statement*.

How to Develop a Growth Mindset

Step 1. *Listen to yourself*

The voice of a fixed mindset will stop you from following the path to success. For example, can you hear yourself questioning whether you have the skills or talent for a project? Do you worry that you'll fail and that people will look down on you? When you think about taking on a new challenge, do you resist for fear of failing? Perhaps you've received negative feedback and you hear yourself making excuses, blaming others and defending yourself. If you do, you can use *thought awareness* to combat negative thinking.

Step 2. *Recognize that you have a choice*

Everyone will face obstacles, challenges and defeats throughout life, but the way that you respond to them can make the difference between success and failure.

If you have a fixed mindset, you'll see these setbacks as proof that you're just not up to the job. But if you look at them as opportunities for growth, you can develop a plan for action, such as learning, working hard, changing your strategy and trying again.

Step 3. *Challenge your fixed mindset*

When you're faced with a challenge and you hear yourself thinking that you'd better not try because you don't have the talent to succeed, remember that you can learn the skills you need to achieve your goals. You may not succeed the first time, but practice will help you to develop. For example, if you're facing a challenge and you think, "I'm not sure I can do this. I don't think I'm smart enough," then challenge this fixed mindset by responding with, "I'm not sure if I can do it and I may not get it right the first time, but I can learn with practice."

Step 4. *Take action.*

When you practice thinking and taking action with a growth mindset, it becomes easier to tackle obstacles in a more positive way. Think of it like practicing the violin: nobody does it perfectly the first time. When you make a mistake, try to see it as a chance to learn.

Think of how you can help your team by using the growth mindset.

Praise your people for their efforts and for having an attitude of learning. If you had a fixed idea of someone's abilities, recognize and appreciate them when they improve. You can support your team's development with workshops or coaching. To build teamwork and encourage people to voice their opinions and ideas, create an environment of open discussion and communication.

Pro - tip: If you have a fixed mindset, try to accept feedback and criticism as opportunities for developing your skills, rather than a judgment of your competence. Be open to learning and less defensive about failing. Remember, everybody makes mistakes!

CHAPTER TWO

LEADERSHIP IN ACTION

> "*Leadership is a process of social influence that maximizes the efforts of others towards the achievement of a goal.- Kevin Kruse*"

Whether you are in a formal leadership position or not, you need to perform certain tasks on a regular basis. So before getting the required skillset, we need to take a look at the tasks performed.

Decision making

> "*"It is in your moments of decision that your destiny is shaped." – Tony Robbins*"

Whether you're a common man or an executive, you need to exercise your decision making capabilities. Some decisions are so simple that you're barely aware you're making them, while others are time-consuming, high risk and can leave you feeling anxious. Decisions can make or break a project or an entire organisation.

At the beginning of 2020, cases of COVID-19 in India were rising gradually. It was a very new thing at the time. The world was suffering from the pandemic and even most of the developed countries like Italy and USA could not manage the crisis. It was speculated that if that pandemic spreads in India with the same rate, India wouldn't be able to manage the number of patients in hospitals.

At that time Prime Minister Narendra Modi took the bold decision and declared a 21-day complete lockdown in the country. Even the railways were stopped for the very first time after the independence of India. Since it was an immediate decision, no one could get time to prepare.

Many people, mostly from marginal section had to depend on donations and social ads for their day to day food. Many people got unemployed. People who earn their wages by doing daily jobs could not do anything as because of lockdown. This abrupt lockdown was highly criticized by opposition parties and some section of the media but when we look back and analyse, it did good for the larger section of people.

Yes, that decision can be easily criticized since some sections of the society faced many problems but at the time, the priority was to save the lives and for saving the lives, even sacrificing our financial well-being and economical growth for sometime is not a big deal.

Exactly the opposite happened in USA. America didn't go for a lockdown and just because of that had to go through the worst crisis in the American history, which exposed the loopholes in its system.

It is not possible to always take the right decisions but you can try to minimize the chances of taking wrong decisions. So is there a process to take better decisions?

Let's look at it. To avoid making a bad decision, you need to bring a range of decision-making skills together in a logical and ordered process. I highly recommend this *7-Step Decision-Making Strategy* for the same.

1. Analyse the situation in detail
2. Develop a productive environment
3. Cultivate reasonable choices
4. Explore your choices
5. Choose the best solution
6. Assess your plan
7. Convey your decision and take action

Let's explore each of these steps in detail.

Step 1: *Analyse the situation in detail.*

Decisions often fail because key factors are missed or ignored from the outset. So before you can begin to make a decision, you need to fully understand your situation.

Start by considering the decision in the context of the problem it is intended to address. You need to determine whether the stated problem is the real issue or just a symptom of something deeper.

Look beyond the obvious. It may be that your objective can be approached in isolation, but it's more likely that there are several interrelated factors to consider. Changes made in one department, for example, could have knock-on effects elsewhere, making the change counter-productive.

Step 2: *Develop a productive environment.*

You should give your decision the time and attention it needs. Spend some time preparing yourself before diving into the facts and figures.

Remember that most decisions will affect other people too, so it helps to create a constructive environment to explore the situation together with all stakeholders and gain support.

This is especially true when you have to rely on other people to implement a decision that you're responsible for. You'll need to identify who to include in the process and who will be the part of any final decision-making group, which will ideally comprise just five to seven people.

Enable people to contribute to the discussions without any fear of the other participants rejecting them and their ideas. Make sure that everyone recognizes that the objective is to make the best decision possible in the circumstances, without blame.

Step 3: *Cultivate reasonable choices.*

The wider the options you explore, the better your final decision is likely to be. Generating some different options may seem to make your decision more complicated at first, but coming up with alternatives forces you to dig deeper and look at the problem from different angles.

This is when it can be helpful to employ a variety of creative thinking techniques. These can help you to step outside your normal patterns of thinking and come up with some truly innovative solutions.

Step 4: *Explore Your Choices*

When you're satisfied that you have a good selection of realistic choices, it's time to evaluate the feasibility, risks and implications of each one.

Almost every decision involves some degree of risk. You'll need a structured approach for assessing threats and evaluating the probability of adverse events occurring and what they might cost to manage. You'll also want to examine the ethical impact of each option, and how that might sit with your personal and organisational values.

Step 5: *Choose the Best Solution*

Once you've evaluated the choices, the next step is to make your decision. You should choose a solution that is beneficial for the maximum number of stakeholders.

Step 6: *Assess your plan.*

After all the effort and hard work you've invested in evaluating and selecting alternatives, it can be tempting to forge ahead at this stage. But now, more than ever is the time to re-assess your decision. After all, it's far better to prevent and repair rather than repent and repair! (*Mark my words*)

Before you start to implement your decision, take a long, dispassionate look at it to be sure that you have been thorough, and that common errors haven't crept into the process.

Discuss your preliminary conclusions with important stakeholders to enable them to spot flaws, make recommendations and support your conclusions. Listen to your intuition too, but quietly and methodically test assumptions and decisions against your own experience.

Step 7: *Convey your decision and take action.*

Once you've made your decision, you need to convey it to everyone affected by it in an engaging, informative and inspiring way. Get them involved in implementing the solution by discussing how and why you arrived at your decision. The more information you provide about risks and projected benefits, the more likely people will be to support it.

If people point out a flaw in your process, have the humility to welcome their input and review your plans appropriately – it's much better to do this now, cheaply, than having to do it expensively (and rather embarrassingly) if your plans have failed.

Team Building

> *"Bigger the dream, more important is the team. - Robin Sharma"*

Human being is a social animal. Most of the time, we work in co-operation with other people. For example, if you are a student, you might need to build your college sports team. If you are a resident living in a colony, you might need to build a team to take care of your housing society.

Nothing great can be accomplished in the materialistic world if you are walking alone. For achieving great results, we need a great team. You don't always get a readymade team. Sometimes, you have to build the team right from a scratch. You have to choose the capable people and train them accordingly. You have to motivate them to make them realise their true potential and pursue a goal.

It was the year 2000 when the Indian cricket team was struck in a match fixing scandal. The fans were angry and Indian cricket was going through its worst phase in the history. In that situation, Sourav Ganguly was appointed as the captain of the Indian cricket team. He started building his team. He gave chances to some inexperienced but talented youngsters like Mohammad Kaif, Yuvraj Singh, Ashish Nehra, Zaheer Khan etc. That team won the ICC Champions Trophy in Sri Lanka and the Natwest trophy in England.

It was the first time that India started winning matches on foreign land. Sourav Ganguly shifted the attitude of team. Although that team could not win the ICC Cricket World Cup in 2003 because the bowling division was not too good at that time, the players nurtured by Sourav Ganguly played a key role in winning the very first ICC World Cup T20 trophy in 2007. Be it MS Dhoni, Yuvraj Singh, Virender Sehwag or Harbhajan Singh, all these players were nurtured by Ganguly. After sometime, these players also contributed in winning the ICC Cricket World Cup in 2011.

Essentials of Team Building

High-performing teams don't materialize out of thin air! They require a very careful cultivation from a team leader with a strong sense of team values, goals and code of conduct. Without this leadership from the top, your employees are simply co-workers. It's up to you to turn them into an actual team. Here are some steps toward making that happen.

1. *Establish expectations from day one.* New team members tend to arrive as relatively blank slates but they will quickly start seeking cues for how to operate as a member of your team. Take advantage of this. Set ground rules and let your expectations be known from the start; not just in terms of the goals but also in terms of the type of team environment you're looking to establish. Do you want to create a culture of shared responsibility, shared problem-solving and shared decision making? If yes, then say so. An effective leader will communicate such values from the very start; this lets new team members understand what they're signing up for.

2. *Respect your team members.* You want your teammates to work in a well co-ordinated way with each other but you must also have another perspective: these are individuals with tales of their own. They have their own rich and varied lives when they leave from work each day. It is important to not regard new team members as bodies who will perform tasks. A robust team environment blossoms when individuals are honoured and respected for their unique gifts and their ability to contribute toward your common goal.
3. *Encourage connections within the team.*It is also important that the team members themselves exhibit some respect and care towards one another. Encourage individuals to regard one another as partners who will work towards a shared goal of community welfare, business development, individual success and achieving team goals.
4. *Practice emotional intelligence.* Great leaders value the importance of emotional intelligence. In a nutshell, this means that their leadership style includes treating individuals as human beings, not machines merely to deliver the desired outcome. Great leaders understand that not every person is motivated by the same thing. Some team players thrive on pursuing shared goals. Others seek healthy competition, either with an outside competitor or against another. By embracing the realities of different work styles and different forms of motivation, an effective leader will treat people's differences as an asset, not an obstacle.
5. *Motivate with positivity.*Great leaders also subscribe to the theory that "you get more flies with honey than vinegar". In real-world terms, this means that it's more effective to shape behaviour with positive

reinforcement rather than negative reinforcement. Resist the urge the criticize team members' mistakes. Instead, create a positive team environment by citing events and behaviours that you particularly liked and encouraging your team to bring more where that came from. Positive reinforcement is a far more productive manner of motivating team performance than shaming those who screwed up.

6. *Communicate.* As humans, we all love to know where we stand. Are my colleagues happy with the work I'm doing? Do I need to improve on something? Assume that people want to know. If they sense you're unhappy but aren't saying anything that can lead up to built-up stress and even resentment, which will result in poor performance. Or if they think they're doing a great job but you, as a boss, aren't satisfied. This can lead to unwelcome shock when you break the news that they've been under-performing. So brush up on those communication skills; effective communication can keep working relationships strong for decades while silence can break things apart very quickly.
7. *Reward good work.* People love recognition of their hard work. If you're fortunate enough to be able to give financial bonuses, it is a great way to show appreciation. If you're in some organisation and a team member shows great judgment, allow them to make some key decisions that you may have once reserved for yourself. Find a small way to show that you're paying close attention to your employees and their efforts are appreciated. It will reflect well on you as a leader, reminding people that they're valued part of the team.
8. *Diversify.* When it comes to building your organisation, your team should be as diverse as possible – different

backgrounds, experiences, ages and opinions. Hire to cover your blind spots: surround yourself with people who will inform you to make the judgment calls on the content you put out.

9. Create. Find a self-starter: someone who can make decisions on your behalf and who's going to be a good ambassador for you and your initiative. Groom them to be collaborators by empowering them to make leadership decisions on their own. You're investing time and resources into this person, so consider their potential for longevity in your team or within your organisation.

Performance enhancement

If you want to lead your organisation in this competitive age, then you must be able to get the very best of each and every one of your team. So part of your job now becomes unleashing the greatness in people who have never seen the greatness within themselves.

Performance enhancement crash course:

1. *Encourage Recognition*

What gets rewarded gets repeated. 96% of the people at workplace accepted that when they receive personal recognition, it definitely inspires and motivates them to do more work. Recognition does inspire people to do more and better work.

Even better, when you create a culture of gratitude and recognition on your team, they will pick it up and start to recognize each other on their own. This creates a great sense of community and cohesion that motivates everyone to perform at their highest level.

2. Create Feedback Loops for Learning and Accountability

All high-performing teams have a learning culture where transparent feedback is crucial for execution. A feedback system always gives chances to find the area of improvements. For all setups, this can be the most appropriate model of working.

3. Lifelong Learning

Leadership is a journey with no real destination. Great leaders commit to continued growth and refinement through continued education, practical application of skills and networking both internally and externally. This includes sharing your knowledge and experiences with others. Commit to developing your team's leadership skills as much as your own and you will find not only gratitude and fulfillment, but will also lay the foundation for a strong leadership pipeline. You see, you are never done growing as a leader!

4. Lead but "Get Out of the Way"

High-performance teams use a decentralized approach to leadership, decision-making and execution. Their leaders have the ability to define the objective, provide the resources and lane markers, and then get out of the way. Team members need free hand and space for creative application of their ideas.

5. Motivating and Inspiring People

We can't inspire others unless we have the idea about the needs of people. *You give them what they want and they will deliver you what you want* is the basic idea behind inspiration. You need to set your example of how you work.

If they see you working hard to pursue your goal then there's also follow you in that path. Motivation doesn't mean just a speech or a lecture. You can't motivate a person only under words. Sometime this can cause more harm. If you always repeat the same words in front of your employee or teammate without knowing their mental condition, they will feel frustrated rather than motivated. So first of all, you must try to understand the mental condition and emotional state. If you are motivating them in a group session then before that session, try to talk to atleast few people individually about their current situation so that you can get a rough idea and you could tackle the situation accordingly.

Strategic planning

> "*A goal is just a dream without a plan. Everything that becomes a success starts with a plan.*"

Strategic planning is an organisational management activity that is used to set priorities, focus energy and resources, strengthen operations, ensure that the employees and other stakeholders are working toward common goals, establish agreement around intended outcomes, and assess and adjust the organisation's direction in response to a changing environment. It is a disciplined effort that produces fundamental decisions and actions that shape and guide what an organisation is, who it serves, what it does, and why it does it, with a focus on the future. Effective strategic planning articulates not only where an organisation is going and the actions needed to make progress, but also how it will know if it is successful.

A strategic plan is a document used to communicate with the organisational team the goals, the actions needed to achieve those goals and all of the other critical elements developed during the planning exercise.

Sometimes, you have to become unconventional to defeat the superior powers. For instance, Chhatrapati Shivaji Maharaj started his kingdom with three forts and later had more than 80 forts. At that time, he had quite a small army but he still got success because he went for unconventional warfare.

He adopted the guerilla warfare techniques and defeated his enemies. Surprise attacks were the main mantra here. Behind the success of Shivaji in his war against cruel Aurangzeb and his allies, it was definitely the unconventional measures taken by him.

Let's break it down into pieces to understand it better.

Step 1: List the Critical Success Factors

Make a comprehensive list of the critical success factors that apply to your organisation or team. These can be divided into two groups: internal factors and external factors. Internal factors can relate to your unit's inherent strengths and weaknesses, whereas external factors can relate to the opportunities and threats in the domain.

For instance, if we talk about a business unit, internal factors could include the maintenance of sufficient production capacity, a strong flow of new technologies from R&D, efficient treasury management and so on. Examples of external success factors will include the rapid adaptation to new government policies, effective competitive analysis and an understanding of the implications of demographic trends.

At this stage, you must try to generate a comprehensive list of the most important critical success factors. This helps to ensure that the key issues are addressed in the comparative analysis process.

Step 2: Assign Weights

Assign a weight to each of these critical success factors, depending on how important it is to the success of your work unit. The higher the importance, the higher weight it will carry. The sum of all weights attached to internal factors should equal 1.0, as should the sum of factors attached to external factors.

Step 3: List the Strategies

Now record the different strategies and approaches that you want to compare.

Step 4: Assign Attractiveness Scores

For each strategy, thoroughly assess the attractiveness of the strategy as it affects each critical success factor. Score each of the CSF (critical success factors) on a scale of 1-4, where the strategy is:

1 = Not attractive at all

2 = Slightly attractive

3 = Attractive

4 = Very attractive

Step 5: Calculate the Weighted Attractiveness Scores

For each Attractiveness Score/Weight combination, calculate the Weighted Attractiveness Score (WAS) by multiplying the weight by the Attractiveness Score (AS) you have assigned for that factor.

Step 6: Sum the Total Attractiveness Scores

This represents the desirability of that particular strategy.

Proper understanding of your vision/goals and common sense are the foundations upon which all this is based. However, it is imperative to note that one must not get into so many technicalities if there are too many things on the platter or if you're heading a small team. Just go with your "gut feeling" or impulses as they call it.

CHAPTER THREE

TRAITS OF GREAT LEADERS

Great leaders make a conscious choice to be a fighter and lead others with their wisdom, knowledge and compassion which will positively impact people. However, no matter what their field of work is, all great leaders have few common traits that make them truly effective.

1. Courage

> "*Courage is the first virtue that makes all other virtues possible. - Aristotle*"

People will wait to see if a leader is courageous before they're willing to follow him or her. People want to see courage in their leaders. They need someone who can make difficult decisions and watch over the good of the group. They need a leader who will stay on course when things get tough. People are far more likely to show courage themselves when their leaders do the same. For the courageous leader adversity is a welcome test.

Leaders who lack courage follow the safest path – the path of least resistance – because they'd rather cover their backside than lead. Courage comes with its rewards which are beyond the thoughts of an ordinary person.

Now here is one clarification. Courage does not mean stupidity. You can't justify acts of foolishness in the name of courage.

It has happened any number of times in our history. One such example is of Chhatrapati Shivaji Maharaj. When he started to emerge as a prominent powerhouse in Maharashtra and Deccan, Delhi's cruel ruler Aurangzeb became quite furious with him. Shivaji Maharaj won many of the forts earlier captured by Mughals and even raised a huge army. So Aurangzeb sent his General with one and a half lakh soldiers to Pune. They captured the town and General Shaista Khan started living in the Lal Mahal, which was childhood days palace of Shivaji.

So Shivaji had two options. One was to fight with the Mughals on the battlefield and the other was to surrender. What did he do?

He chose the path of extraordinary courage with a blend of intelligence! He raided the Lal Mahal secretly with a few hundred soldiers at night on 5th April, 1663. In this raid the Mughal General Shaista Khan lost his fingers. Due to the chaos created in the palace, the larger but confused Mughal army ran away. Due to great humilation, Shaista Khan shifted his camp to Aurangabad. Mughal emperor Aurangzeb became unpleasent over this unprecedent defeat.

Chhatrapati Shivaji took a calculated risk with a well structured plan. His courage paid off and recaptured the Pune once again.

2. Integrity

> *"Integrity is not a bunch of values or ethics. It is the coherence between how you are, how you think, and how you act. - Sadhguru"*

Integrity is a characteristic that many of us value in ourselves and it is one we definitely look for in our leaders. But what does it really mean to have integrity?

Some of the dictionary definitions of integrity are:

- Adherence to moral and ethical principles
- Soundness of moral character; honesty
- The state of being whole, entire or undiminished
- A sound, unimpaired or perfect condition

Although the definition is sound, it can be a bit more complex to define integrity in our everyday lives.

You could say that integrity is always doing the right thing, even when no one is looking and even when the choice isn't easy. Or, you might see integrity as staying true to yourself and your word, even when you're faced with serious consequences for the choices that you're making.

When we have integrity, we're whole and in perfect condition, and we're not compromised by awkward inconsistencies.

When we live our lives with integrity, it means that we're always honest, and we let our actions speak for who we are and what we believe in. Integrity is a choice we make, and it's a choice we must keep making, every moment of our lives.

When Mahatma Gandhi started non-cooperation movement against British government, it was going well, but unfortunately police fired at a mob in Chauri Chaura. In retaliation to this, the mob set the police station on fire, killing 23 policemen. It was against Gandhi's idea of non-violence. It was against his core values so he immediately rolled back the non-cooperation movement despite the fact that it was gaining momentum.

There are several reasons why integrity is so important. First, living a life of integrity means that we never have to spend time or energy questioning ourselves. When we listen to our hearts and do the right thing, life becomes simple. Our lives, and our actions, are open for everyone to see and we don't have to worry about hiding anything. When we have integrity, we gain the trust of our leaders, our colleagues and our team. We're dependable, and when we hold ourselves accountable for our actions, we become role models for others to follow.

All of this, in turn, directly impacts our success in life. People who live and work with integrity are more likely to be considered for promotions.

Why? Because integrity is a hallmark of trust. Organisations want leaders that they can trust, and when you demonstrate integrity, you show everyone you can be trusted.

> "*The reputation of a thousand years may be determined by the conduct of one hour.*"

Your integrity is what determines your reputation and just as this proverb states, all it can take is a single bad choice to destroy a lifetime's worth of integrity.

So, how can you work on developing and preserving your own integrity?

Step 1: *Define Your Values*

You can't live by values if you don't know what you truly believe in. So, start by defining your core values. These are the values that, no matter what the consequence, you're not going to compromise on.

Step 2: *Analyse Every Choice You Make*

Often, people cut corners or make bad choices when they think there's no one watching. Having integrity means that, no matter what; you make the right choice, especially when no one is watching!

You'll usually know what's right and wrong, although sometimes you might need some quiet time to figure it out. If you're not sure what the right choice is, ask yourself these two questions:

1. If my choice was printed on the front page of the newspaper for everyone to see, would I feel okay about it?
2. If I make this choice, will I feel okay with myself afterwards?

Remember, honesty and integrity aren't values that you should live by when it's convenient; they're values that you should live by all the time. This includes the big choices and the little choices – the choices everyone sees, and the choices that no one sees!

Step 3: *Encourage Integrity*

People with integrity often have the same characteristics: they're humble, they have high self-esteem, and they're self-confident. These characteristics are important, because, sometimes, you'll be under intense pressure from others to make the wrong choice.

Work on building and improving these characteristics within yourself, so that you have the strength and courage to do the right thing when the time comes. Build your self-confidence and self-esteem and work on developing character. Spend time getting to know yourself and what you believe in. Develop friendships and work relationships with others who demonstrate integrity, and those who will support your decisions.

There are few more tips one can make use of in order to nurture their integrity:

- Learn how to be assertive, so that you can defend an ethical position from an adult point of view, without whining or being aggressive.
- Avoid white lies. They may seem harmless, but tiny lies are still lies. Always tell the truth.
- Learn to take responsibility for your actions. If you make a mistake, own up to it immediately and do whatever it takes to right the situation.
- Keep your word, and don't make promises that you know you can't keep.
- Keep in mind that in times of fear, disaster and chaos, the temptation is even greater to make a wrong choice. Use these opportunities to demonstrate your true character.
- Stay humble and down-to-earth, don't look for approval and where you sensibly can, try to let people save face.

3. Generosity

> *"A good leader is a person who takes a little more than his share of the blame and a little less than his share of the credit. – John Maxwell"*

Great leaders are generous. They share credit and offer enthusiastic praise. They're as committed to their followers' success as they are to their own. They want to inspire all the employees to achieve their personal best – not just because it will make the team more successful, but because they care about each person as an individual.

The late A.P.J. Abdul Kalam liked telling stories with morals. A story he was particularly fond of, was related to the launch of a satellite by the Indian Space Research Organisation in July 1979. Kalam was in charge of the project at ISRO and when some members expressed reservations about its readiness, he overruled them and ordered it to go ahead. The launch failed; instead of going into space, the satellite plunged into the Bay of Bengal. As team leader, Kalam was humiliated by the failure and terrified by the prospect of announcing it before the press. He was saved from embarrassment by the chairman of ISRO, Satish Dhawan, who himself went before the television cameras to say that despite the failure, he reposed complete faith in the abilities of his team and was confident that their next attempt would succeed.

The following August, Kalam and his team tried once more to launch a satellite into space. This time they succeeded. Dhawan congratulated the team, while asking Kalam to address the press conference. In telling the story in later years, during and after his term as president of India, Kalam would feelingly recall: "*When the failure occurred, the leader owned it up. When the success came, he gave the credit to his team.*"

4. Vision

"Vision is the art of seeing what is invisible to others. - Jonathan Swift"

True leaders have a vision, that is, they have a potential to view the present as it is and to invent a future culminating out of the present. A leader with a vision can foresee the future and can remain in the present. A vision is an end towards which leader can spend and direct his energy and resources. Leaders share a dream and a path which the employees want to share and follow. Leadership vision is not restricted to a written organisational mission statement and vision statement. It is well demonstrated in the actions, beliefs and values of organisational leaders.

If there is no vision, people cannot survive. This is applicable both in business as well as in life. Leaders who lack vision cannot succeed in life and they work in a typical monotonous manner.

Vision is not a fantasy for leaders; rather it is a truth that is yet to come into practice. So as to achieve vision, a leader must exert special extra efforts and have robust confidence and devotion to realise the vision.

Vision acts as an internal force propelling a leader to act. It provides an objective to the leader. The consistent existence of a vision makes a leader progressive despite various hardships and obstacles. Vision is a bond that unites the individuals into team with a mutual goal.

This is the major difference between management and leadership which is not only managing the day-to-day tasks but at the same time, keep thinking about the future. They learn from their experiences of the past, prepare for the future and take action in present.

Let us revert back to the life story of one of the greatest rulers of India to learn about how a visionary man build an independent empire from scratch. The man was Chhatrapati Shivaji, who was born on 19 February 1630 to Shahaji Bhonsle, a Maratha general serving the Deccan sultanates and Jijabai, the daughter of Lakhuji Jadhavrao of Sindhkhed, a descendant from a Yadav royal family of Devagiri. It was a time when the Mughal power were at its zenith, ruling over much of India while Muslim sultans held sway over the Deccan from Bijapur and Golconda. From an early age itself, the flames of regaining 'Hindavi Swaraj' (self-rule of Indians) was flickering in the mind of young Shivaji. His mother was his mentor, who taught him Indian values and about dharma and to fight injustice. She read to him the sacred texts of the Ramayana and Mahabharata and infused in him the pride of his people through stories of the brave Hindu Kings and Queens who had fought invasions for centuries. Thus young Shivaji grew up, imbued with a dream and a vision of creating a nation free from foreign rule.

Before the age of twenty he had captured four forts, without an army and without a battle! The word of his successes spread across neighbouring villages like wildfire, injecting hope and excitement among all. Soon, Shivaji had an eager army of about three hundred village lads, who left behind their books and sickles to be with him. These young men had never held a weapon and were innocent to warfare, but then, Shivaji was a man who could inspire men to have hoped again and to fight for the impossible. And it is from such humble beginnings that he raised a great army and navy.

Behind the seemingly effortless campaigns and successes of Shivaji, lay the sharp mind of a strategist. He closely studied his enemies and tactically played them against each other as in the case of the Mughals and the Bijapur Sultanate. Shivaji's vision was characterized by a deep understanding of the strengths and capabilities of his opponents along with a practical realization of the limits of his own power at the time. In present-day parlance, his tactics could well be referred to as 'asymmetric warfare'. He avoided battle on the plains where his forces would obviously be outnumbered and defeated, and took the battle to the hills where his limited troops stood chance to defeat a vastly superior force.

His ambush of Shaista Khan is the stuff that legends are made of! As the viceroy of the Deccan, Khan had arrived with a huge army to capture Shivaji. Displaying great personal courage and impeccable planning, Shivaji turned the tables on him. With a few hundred men, he entered the courtyard of Khan's palace through subterfuge, and raided the place. Shaista Khan's son, along with many of his soldiers, was killed in the attack. He himself narrowly escaped after losing three of his fingers. This left the Khan in disgrace, and Shivaji's legendary status was further enhanced.

Due to his sharp instincts, Shivaji was always two steps ahead of his enemies, which helped him neutralize foes like the Adil Shahi General, Afzal Khan. The story of his concealed armour and the *bagh-nukh* has thrilled and inspired children and adults alike for generations. But Shivaji was never led by bravado and sacrifice alone. At the root of each of his endeavours, lay the grand vision of *Hindavi Swaraj* and to achieve that goal, he had the courage and self-confidence to retreat when the odds were not in his favour. In the larger scheme of things, it was more important to live to fight another day. Thus he accepted the Treaty of Purandhar, which cost him the loss of around 20 forts, leaving him with just a dozen. But that was better than losing them all, for, a temporary setback was one he could recover from. And as history informs us, Shivaji did win back all his forts.

An astute warrior, Shivaji knew the importance of speed and tactics in the battle. The guerrilla warfare of his highly disciplined infantry was menacing for his enemies. And his lightning fast cavalry was trained to ride for long hours. The men sustained themselves on two small meals a day. Perhaps that is why he could keep on singlehandedly fighting both the European enterprises and the Mughals. Alongside the battles, he continued with his diplomatic forays, signing treaties with even those who were sent to annihilate him. With each success, his power and influence grew.

As a young boy, Shivaji had taken the scattered Maratha hill-folk and turned them into a swift and agile army. As a King, he established a state that set the foundation of the Grand Maratha Empire. For all administrative purposes, he set up an advisory council of ministers knows as the *asht-pradhan.* His revenue system was robust and made concessions for the times of famine. His justice system was swift and sure, with no tolerance for crimes and in all this, he remained an approachable King.

And above all, much-loved one as well. In the words of J.N. Sarkar, "He welded the Marathas into a mighty nation."

In a world that blindly celebrates conquerors that destroy foreign cultures and nations, Shivaji stands out for the love of his motherland... For he was a man resisting the rapacious destruction and invasion of his land, culture and people. When large parts of India were under the oppressive rule of Aurangzeb, the proud standard of the

Maratha Empire flew in the Deccan and filled the hearts of millions with hope and pride. Campaign after campaign of the Mughal dynasty against Shivaji failed. Eventually, Aurangzeb had to grudgingly acknowledge him as King and even sent him gifts on his coronation. Shivaji, the simple hill boy had battled the Europeans and the Mughals all alone. And with his foresight, bravery and love for *Swaraj*, shared the idea of a self-rule for his beloved motherland.

Chhtarapati Shivaji had a vision of Hindavi Swaraj, around which he gathered his team. Moreover his men recognized his vision and they were always ready to put efforts upto any extent to realize that vision into reality

On the same note, recognition of a leader's vision by the organisational team is also very essential as it makes them well aware of what the organisation is trying to achieve. Vision has the strength to move the team members out of monotonous routines and goal-chasing and place them in challenging and dynamic work.

Vision must be:

- Rational
- Reasonable
- Innovative
- Credible
- Clear
- Motivating and stimulating
- Challenging
- Reflective of organisational beliefs, values and culture
- Concrete

It is a leader who moulds, interprets, communicates and represents the vision. Vision is a portrait and depiction of what a leader aspires his organisation to be in the long-run.

5. *Proactive*

This simply means, taking action for causing a positive change and not only reacting to change when it happens.

Situations will arise and reactive mass will simply react to it whereas responsible people will respond as per the demands of the situation. Many people are waiting for invitations that only when someone asks them to do something, they will do, otherwise, they will not do anything.

So what being proactive means is that one is ready to take initiative and plunge into action according to the circumstances. It is a wonderful but rare quality which is very hard to find in the world today. Leaders are always proactive!

For example, suppose a person you don't know has met with a serious accident in your street. Most of the people will think why to bother themselves since they don't know the guy. Everyone gathers around the spot but no one is trying to help the person affected. Suddenly, your friend rushes in through the crowd and starts nursing this wounded person. All of a sudden, what happens is that some other people also approach to help them out. Had your friend not taken the initiative, no one might have dared to come forward. This attribute is called being proactive and is one of the foremost quality which makes leaders stand apart from that their followings.

A famous incident is one related to Mahatma Gandhi when he was going by a train in South Africa. Suddenly, a British man abused him for traveling in the first class coach "reserved for the whites" and just threw his luggage and Mr Gandhi out of the coach. That was the thing after which

Mahatma Gandhi started Satyagraha in South Africa itself. While this was not a new thing in South Africa, no one cared to stand up for their rights. Gandhiji did not start the Satyagraha just because he was insulted. He actually thought that it's about injustice and fundamental human rights. That's why, he took the initiative and forced the mighty British government to change the rules which was not at all easy in the given time and era of the oppressive British Raj.

So now let's see how can you become proactive because practical application is what makes the maximum difference.

- Try to take on different roles. Don't assume they already have someone else for that new project or task that interests you. Chances are you don't need a Masters and a PHD for tasks outside your assigned work. If you ask for additional responsibility, there's a good chance you will receive it.
- Ask for feedback and act on it. Not only will you improve yourself, but your team leaders and co-workers will have a new standard to benchmark your growth and progress against.
- Make an effort to listen to discussions around you. Do this even if they are irrelevant to your work. This is a great way to learn about new opportunities you could capitalize on.
- Don't underestimate the power of small-talk. There are many interesting and motivated people around you and there is always a lot to learn from them. Take advantage of this and watch your skills build.
- Don't be shy to ask questions. If you want to take initiative, the only option is to ask questions and

understand how things work. It's more effective to learn from others who have been in your shoes before, than to try and do it alone.

- Don't take comments and suggestions personally. Your fellow team members aren't questioning your capabilities; they are providing you with constructive feedback that help you reach your potential. Learn to love feedback as it's the key to improving.
- Have a positive outlook. Complaining is far from constructive if you believe a process or method needs to change. With a positive attitude, you can work towards the change and make an impact.
- Taking initiative may make you feel uncomfortable since you'll often be forced to step outside your comfort zone, but why not get comfortable with being uncomfortable and be one step ahead? Challenge yourself to take initiative and be proactive today!

6. *Adaptability*

> "*The most important factor in survival is neither intelligence nor strength but adaptability. - Charles Darwin*"

The world has become so dynamic since we are going through an era of rapid changes. When I was 15 years old, only a handful of people had phone. Now, almost every person carries a smart-phone.

Similarly, online education was a less-preferred alternative before 2020, but the rise of Corona cases made this thing a prevalent reality. So many things become irrelevant so quickly. If you are not adaptable, after sometime, you will become irrelevant and irrelevant people cannot lead in the world.

To quote an example, let's talk about one of the greatest Show-Man of Indian politics, PM Narendra Modi. He started using Twitter and other social media for public interaction and was ahead of his counterparts in adopting technology. He identified the potential of social media in changing times and leveraged it in his political campaigns.

Let's talk about how can one become adaptable...

- Learn from others' mistakes.
- Ask questions, expand your comfort zone and learn new skills.
- Open up your mindset, always keep changing and be in pace with the world.

7. Resilience

> "*More than education, more than experience, more than training, a person's level of resilience will determine who succeeds and who fails.*"

Resilience is the capacity to recover quickly from challenges. Sometimes life becomes difficult. We try taking steps to improve the situations, but all in vain. Life is unpredictable, and the journey often takes us in unexpected directions. The key here is not to give up and do whatever best is possible. Let us look at how it can happen in real life...

3rd April 2016, Kolkata, Finals of the ICC World Cup T20 (England v West Indies)

West Indies needed 19 runs in the last over. The ball was in the hands of Ben Stokes. It was looking an easy victory for England. Carlos Brathwaite smashed Ben Stokes for four consecutive sixes in the last over of the World 2020 finals with 19 runs to win.

After the fourth six, Stokes crouched on the pitch, head in hands, shattered. He had done the job of a death bowler well throughout the tournament, but the night when it mattered the most, the night where he could help his country win an ICC Trophy, he had given it away! This was the first watershed moment of his career. Such a thrashing is usually enough to end a promising career as the player is just not able to recover from the trauma. However, Stokes was stronger. He knew he had it in him to turn things around. Little did he know, Kolkata was not when his career came closest to being ended. It was Bristol.

Bristol, 2017

On 25 September 2017, Ben Stokes was arrested for allegedly punching a man outside a bar after being intoxicated. He was banned for eight matches.

Stokes could see a career, which had just started to take shape in the way he wanted, slip away, once and for all. His antics off the field had often clouded his on-field performances. Questions were posed time and time again, whether Ben Stokes really took his cricket seriously.

Everyone had come to believe, Ben Stokes was the big bad guy of cricket and irrespective of his good performances, he would never earn the respect of the people. But Stokes fought to live another day.

On 7 December 2019, almost 15 months later, Stokes was declared not guilty.

It was revealed he had actually taken a stand against homophobic abuse being dished to two other men that night. Had it been an ordinary player he would have lost his faith in himself.

July 2019, Finals of the ICC Cricket World Cup at Lord's (New Zealand v England)

One moment of impulse also changed his life forever. With 9 needed off 3 balls in the tightly contested World Cup final, Stokes smashed the ball towards the leg side which seemed was going to be a single, but Stokes came rushing back for the second, and at the moment he dived. In a final bid to make his ground, the ball, thrown in by Martin Guptill, ricocheted off his bat and away from all the New Zealand fielders to the boundary.

The English team was awarded 6 runs. Stokes had his hands up in the air as if to say it wasn't his fault, this time.

The last ball, with 2 to win saw Stokes, now a completely transformed individual, realizing how fortunate he was to be able to represent England, tapped a full toss for a single, instead of trying to go for the glory shot. This incredibly took the final of the World Cup to a super-over, which as we all know, ended with England emerging victorious. Ben Stokes, the man who had only been known as a *villain*, an image he didn't bother rectifying either, was England's biggest hero.

"I want to do things on the field, to be remembered for. If we win the World Cup, that becomes the first paragraph, doesn't it? I don't want to be remembered as the guy who had a fight in the street." Stokes had said before the World Cup. He made sure he got his first paragraph!

But he didn't stop there. The World Cup summer was soon to be transformed into Ben Stokes' summer. He also contributed to England getting multiple victories in the subsequent months and years, culminating in him receiving the honour of leading the English Test team.

Steps to build resilience:

- Accepting

The first step in dealing with adversity is acceptance. Resilient people accept that suffering is part of life, and adversity doesn't discriminate. They understand that those perfect lives portrayed in movies aren't reality. Acceptance isn't about giving up and letting our suffering take over. It's about confronting the full range of our emotions and trusting that we will bounce back.

- *Reframing*

At the simplest level, it's changing perspectives–changing the way you look at something or trying to understand whatever you're seeing or involved in. Usually we see the things only one way. Try to look at the situation from different perspective. Look at change as an opportunity rather than something to fear. For example, if you'vc just lost your job, now may be the perfect time to consider a career change.

- *Acknowledging*

Being able to switch the focus of your attention to not just focus on the bad but also acknowledge the good is crucial. When you focus too much on the most stressful areas of your life, you forget to recognize what's going right. It's about breaking the cycle of negativity so you can be grateful for the positive things in your life.

- *Focusing*

Truly resilient people are able to focus on what they can change and ignore what they can't. Attempt to evaluate your level of control over a situation. Ask yourself, "What can I take responsibility for?" Accepting circumstances that can't be changed can help you focus on conditions that you can alter. When you look for opportunities to empower yourself, you're less likely to feel stuck and helpless.

- *Evaluating*

In Lucy Hone's impactful Tedx talk, "The Three secrets of resilient people" she describes a powerful strategy for dealing with adversity. Ask yourself this question, "Is what I'm doing helping or harming me?" Personally, I've found this to be a life-changing exercise. When you're about to eat that extra piece of your favourite sweet dish or realize your exercise routine is virtually non-existent, ask yourself, "Is this helping or harming me?" You will inevitably get an answer that will benefit you in the long run. This practice puts you back in control over your decision making—turning you into a survivor rather than a victim.

CHAPTER FOUR

SKILLSET FOR A LEADER

I. *Emotional Intelligence*

Emotional Intelligence is the term popularized by Daniel Goleman. In his phenomenal work *Emotional Intelligence*, he has defined the emotions. Today many psychologists and social scientists believe that emotional intelligence plyas a crucial role in developing one's personality.

If we understand in simple terms, our brain can be looked as divided into two parts as emotional brain and logical brain. The emotional brain is fast in responding and takes command when some external triggers stimulate our mind. When emotional brain takes the helm, our logical reasoning reduces drastically.

There are any number of instances of a highly intelligent and skilled executive, who was promoted into a leadership position only to fail at the job. And there are also stories of someone with solid, but not extraordinary intellectual abilities and technical skills, who was promoted into a similar position and then soared.

Such anecdotes support the widespread belief that identifying individuals with the "right stuff" to be leaders is more art than science. After all, the personal styles of superb leaders vary: some leaders are subdued and analytical while others shout their manifestos from the mountaintops. And just as important, different situations call for different types of leadership. Most mergers need a sensitive negotiator at the helm, whereas many turnarounds require a more forceful authority.

According to Daniel Goleman, a stalwart in the field of emotional intelligence, the most effective leaders are alike in one crucial way: they all have a high degree of what has come to be known as emotional intelligence. It's not that IQ and technical skills are irrelevant. They do matter, but mainly as "threshold capabilities"; that is, they are the entry-level requirements for executive positions. But Goleman's research and studies clearly showed that emotional intelligence is the main thing of leadership. Without it, a person can have the best training in the world, an incisive, analytical mind and an endless supply of smart ideas, but he still won't make a great leader.

As per Daniel Goleman, it is emotional intelligence (EI): a group of five skills that enable the best leaders to maximize their own and their followers' performance. When senior managers at one company had a critical mass of EI capabilities, their divisions outperformed yearly earnings goals by 20%.

These EI skills are:

• Self-awareness – knowing one's strengths, weaknesses, drives, values and impact on others.

• Self-regulation – controlling or redirecting disruptive impulses and moods.

• Motivation – relishing achievement for its own sake.

• Empathy – understanding the emotional makeup of other people.

• Social skills – establishing rapport with others to move them in desired directions.

We're all born with certain levels of EI skills. But we can strengthen these abilities through persistence, practice and feedback from colleagues or coaches. The only key is to have the desire to learn and grow.

Moreover, Goleman's analysis showed that emotional intelligence played an increasingly important role at the highest levels of the company, where differences in technical skills are of negligible importance. In other words, the higher the rank of a person considered being a star performer, the more emotional intelligence capabilities showed up as the reason for his or her effectiveness. When he compared star performers with average ones in senior leadership positions, nearly 90% of the difference in their profiles was attributable to emotional intelligence factors rather than cognitive abilities.

Other researchers have confirmed that emotional intelligence not just distinguishes outstanding leaders, but can also be linked to strong performance. In short, the numbers are beginning to tell us a persuasive story about the link between a company's success and the emotional intelligence of its leaders. And just as important, research is also demonstrating that people can, if they take the right approach, develop their emotional intelligence.

Let us look at the five key emotional intelligence skills that Goleman talked about in detail and understand how one can incorporate them in the daily lives to become an impactful leader in all our endeavours.

Self-Awareness

Definition – the ability to recognize and understand your moods, emotions and drives as well as their effect on others.

Hallmark – self-confidence, realistic self-assessment, self-deprecating sense of humour.

Suppose you are holding a meeting with your team mates. You are not happy with the work of one of your teammates and get angry with her performance. Emotions are far more powerful than your logical thinking. You might say something in the anger that can lead to a disastrous outcome. Your image may get maligned in a second. But if you are aware of your thoughts and your emotions, then you can do something to control it. So self-awareness is the very first step in becoming emotional intelligent.

It's like a fire alarm alerting your house. Whenever fire-like situation arises at some place in your house, then it just informs you timely so that you can take anticipatory action. Those who are self aware know what triggers them and what drives them so they are not dependent on external situations to make them happy. They can diagnose the real reason behind their mood swings.

It is the skill to keep yourself at some distance from your emotions so that emotion could not overwhelm you. As we observe in our daily life, situations become harmful because we are not aware of it.

People with strong self-awareness are neither overly critical nor unrealistically hopeful. Rather, they are honest, with themselves and with others.

People who have a high degree of self-awareness recognize how their feelings affect them, other people and their job performance. Thus, a self- aware person who knows that tight deadlines bring out the worst in him plans his time carefully and gets his work done well in advance. Another person with high self-awareness will be able to work with a demanding client. She will understand the client's impact on her moods and the deeper reasons for her frustration. And she will go one step further and turn her anger into something constructive.

Self-awareness extends to a person's understanding of his or her values and goals. Someone who is highly self-aware knows where he is headed and why. For example, he will be able to be firm in turning down a job offer that is tempting financially but does not fit with his principles or long-term goals. A person who lacks self-awareness is apt to make decisions that bring on inner turmoil by treading on buried values. "The money looked so good, but this job has ruined my life." So many people are found saying this two years into the job. The decisions of self-aware people mesh with their values and consequently, they often find work to be energizing.

How can one recognize self-awareness? First and foremost, it shows itself as sincerity and an ability to assess oneself realistically. People with high self-awareness are able to speak accurately and openly, although not necessarily effusively or confessionally, about their emotions and the impact they have on their work.

Such self-knowledge often shows itself in the hiring process also. Ask a candidate to describe a time he got carried away by his feelings and did something he later regretted. Self-aware candidates will be frank in admitting to failure and will often tell their tales with a smile. One of the main hallmarks of self-awareness is a self-deprecating sense of humor.

Self-awareness can also be identified during performance reviews. Self-aware people know, and are comfortable talking about, their limitations and strengths and they often demonstrate a thirst for constructive criticism. By contrast, people with low self-awareness interpret the message that they need to improve as a threat or a sign of failure.

Self-aware people can also be recognized by their self-confidence. They have a firm grasp of their capabilities and are less likely to set themselves up to fail by, for example, overstretching on any of the assignments. They also know when to ask for help. And the risks they take on the job are calculated. They won't ask for a challenge that they know they can't handle alone. They'll always play to their strengths.

Despite the value of having self-aware people in the workplace, many researches indicate that senior executives don't often give self-awareness the credit it deserves when they look for potential leaders. Many executives mistake honesty about feelings for 'wimpiness' and fail to give due respect to employees who openly acknowledge their shortcomings. Such people are too readily dismissed as "not tough enough" to lead others. In fact, the opposite is true. In the first place, people generally admire and respect truthfulness. Furthermore, leaders are constantly required to make judgment calls that require a candid assessment of capabilities – their own and those of others. People who assess themselves honestly are well suited to do the same for the organisations they run.

Always thinking about the past and future diminishes our prospects of being well. If you are fully focused on the present moment itself, then we can enhance the degree of self-awareness.

A simple process of writing your emotions can simply change the course of your life. At the end of the day, write down when did you become angry, what caused it etc can really help you becoming aware of your emotions.

Self-Regulation

Definition – the ability to control or redirect impulses and moods or simply the ability to think before acting.

Hallmark – trustworthiness and integrity, comfort with ambiguity, openness to change.

After self-awareness, the next step of self-governance is self-regulation and channelizing our emotions to command the behaviour and moulding it gradually.

Biological impulses drive our emotions. We cannot do away with them, but we can do much to manage them. Self-regulation, which is like an ongoing inner conversation, is the component of emotional intelligence that frees us from being prisoners of our feelings. People engaged in such a conversation feel bad moods and emotional impulses just as everyone else does, but they find ways to control them and even to channel them in useful ways.

Imagine an executive who has just watched a team of his employees present a botched analysis to the company's board of directors. In the gloom that follows, the executive might find himself tempted to pound on the table in anger or kick over a chair. He could leap up and scream at the group. Or he might maintain a grim silence, glaring at everyone before stalking off.

But if he had a gift for self-regulation, he would choose a different approach.

He would pick his words carefully, acknowledging the team's *not-so-good* performance without rushing to any hasty judgment. He would then step back to consider the reasons for the failure. Are they personal – due to someone's lack of effort? Are there any mitigating factors? What was his role in the debacle? After considering these questions, he would call the team together, lay out the incident's consequences and offer his feelings about it. He would then present his analysis of the problem and a well-considered solution.

Why does self-regulation matter so much for leaders? First of all, people who are in reasonable control of their feelings and impulses are able to create an environment of trust and fairness where politics and infighting are sharply reduced and productivity is high. Talented people flock to the organisation and aren't tempted to leave. And self-regulation has a trickle-down effect. No one wants to be known as a hot-head when the boss is known for her calm approach. Fewer bad moods at the top usually also mean fewer throughout the organisation.

Secondly, self-regulation is important for competitive reasons. Everyone knows that all industries are rife with ambiguity and change. Companies merge and break apart regularly. Technology transforms work at a dizzying pace. People who have mastered their emotions are able to move with the changes. When a new program is announced, they don't panic; instead, they are able to suspend judgment, seek out information, and listen to the executives as they explain the new program. As the initiative moves forward, these people are able to move with it. Sometimes they even lead the way.

Consider the case of a manager at a large manufacturing company. Like her colleagues, she had used a certain data collection software program for five years. The program drove how she thought about the company's strategy. One day, senior executives announced that a new program was to be installed that would radically change how information was gathered and assessed within the organisation. While many people in the company complained bitterly about how disruptive the change would be, the manager mulled over the reasons for the new program and was convinced of its potential to improve performance. She eagerly attended training sessions and was eventually promoted to run several divisions, in part because she used the new technology so effectively.

I want to push the importance of self-regulation to leadership even further and make the case that it enhances integrity, which is not only a personal virtue but also an organisational strength. Many of the bad things that happen in companies are a function of impulsive behavior.

Consider the behavior of a senior executive at a large food company who was conscientiously honest in his dealings with local distributors. He would routinely lay out his cost structure in detail, thereby giving the distributors a reasonable understanding of the company's pricing. This approach meant he couldn't always drive a hard bargain. Once, he felt the urge to increase profits by withholding certain information about the company's costs. But he defied that impulse! He saw that it made more sense in the long-run to counteract it. His emotional self-regulation paid off in strong, lasting relationships with distributors that benefited the company more than any short-term financial gains would have.

The signs of emotional self-regulation, therefore, are easy to see: a propensity for reflection and thoughtfulness, comfort with ambiguity and change and integrity which is an ability to say no to impulsive urges. However, like self-awareness, self-regulation often does not get its due.

People who can master their emotions are sometimes seen as cold fish—their considered responses are taken as a lack of passion.

People with fiery temperaments are often thought of as *classic* leaders. Their outbursts are considered hallmarks of charisma and power. But when such people make it to the top, their impulsiveness often works against them.

Motivation

Definition – a passion to work for reasons that go beyond money or status and pursue goals with energy and persistence.

Hallmark – strong drive to achieve, optimism even when faced with failure, organisational commitment.

If there is one trait that nearly all effective leaders have, it is motivation. They are driven to achieve beyond their own and everyone else's expectations. The key word here is *achieve*. Plenty of people are motivated by external factors, such as a big salary or the status that comes from having an impressive title or being part of a prestigious company. By contrast, those with leadership potential are motivated by a deeply embedded desire to achieve for the sake of achievement.

If you are looking for leaders, how can you identify people who are motivated by the drive to achieve rather than by external rewards? The first sign is a passion for the work itself; such people seek out creative challenges, love to learn and take great pride in a job well done. They also display an unflagging energy to do things better. People with such energy often seem restless with the status quo. They are persistent with their questions about why things are done one way rather than another; they are eager to explore new approaches to their work.

As an educator, I Have observed that students don't lake hard work or intelligence but they lake motivation. Every time they write test, they wish to have good marks but when they don't get, they become frustrated. They lose their motivation. A demotivated person can't put his 100% efforts. It happened with me when I was in college. In a semester exam, I was determined to get very good marks but I could not get due to some reasons and I become so disappointed that in the very next semester my performance fall drastically. I scored worst of my entire student life in that semester.

That story illustrates two other common traits of people who are driven to achieve. They are forever raising the performance bar, and they like to keep score.

During performance reviews, people with high levels of motivation might ask to be *stretched* by their superiors. Of course, an employee who combines self-awareness with internal motivation will recognize her limits – but she won't settle for objectives that seem too easy to fulfill. People who are driven to do better, essentially, want a way of tracking progress of each team member, including their own. While people with low achievement motivation are often fuzzy about results, those with high achievement motivation often keep score by tracking.

Interestingly, people with high motivation remain optimistic even when the score is against them. In such cases, self-regulation combines with achievement motivation to overcome the frustration and depression that come after a setback or failure.

It may sound a bit strange but people who don't care much about the end outcomes have a better chance to feel always motivated. *Love your work also not the end outcome only.*

If you set the performance bar high for yourself, you will do the same for the organisation when you are in a position to do so. Likewise, a drive to surpass goals and an interest in keeping score can be contagious. And of course, optimism and organisational commitment are fundamental to leadership.

Empathy

Definition – the ability to understand the emotional make-up of other people and treating them according to their emotional reactions.

Hallmark – expertise in building and retaining talent, cross-cultural sensitivity, service to clients and customers.

Of all the dimensions of emotional intelligence, empathy is the most easily recognized. We have all felt the empathy of a sensitive teacher or friend; we have all been struck by its absence in an unfeeling coach or boss.

But empathy doesn't mean a kind of "I'm OK, you're OK" mushiness. For a leader, it doesn't mean adopting other people's emotions as one's own and trying to please everybody. That would be a nightmare! It would make action impossible. Rather, empathy means thoughtfully considering the feelings of all team members, along with other factors, in the process of making intelligent decisions.

Imagine you are a student and a friend in your class has just failed a major test or exam. Your friend is distraught because she studied really hard and still failed. Even though you got a good grade on this test, you remember what it is like to fail. You don't try to fix things for your friend. Instead, you make an empathetic statement like, "I'm so, so sorry about your grade. I know how hard you studied and how disappointed you must feel."

Empathy is different from sympathy. Having empathy for someone means that you can feel the pain and frustration that they are feeling, and probably have felt similar feelings in your own life. These are normal human emotions and they are normally triggered in the people nearby. When you show empathy for another person, you are treating them as a peer who you are concerned about and can relate to as an equal in distress

There are several reasons that make empathy a core competency for truly effective leaders :

Trust: Being able to demonstrate empathy creates trust within your team.Trust creates an empowering, honest relationship with yourcolleagues. In turn, this will increase collaboration and productivity,but most importantly your team will be assured that their feelingsare being taken care of.

Presence: Empathy also cultivates a greater presence in your leadership role.

Multiple responsibilities can be difficult and distracting, so demonstrating empathy allows you to increase your attentiveness and teach you how to be patient.

Communication: If you're able to demonstrate empathy, people will feel safe talkingto you. It will allow you to listen and have a clearer picture of how toeffectively manage your team.

Consider the challenge of leading a team. As anyone who has ever been a part of one can attest, teams are kettles of bubbling emotions. They are often charged with reaching a consensus, which is hard enough with two people and much more difficult as the numbers increase. Even in groups with as few as four or five members, alliances form and clashing agendas get set. A team leader must be able to sense and understand the viewpoints of everyone around the table.

That's exactly what a marketing manager at a large information technology company was able to do when she was appointed to lead a troubled team. The group was in turmoil, overloaded by work and missing deadlines.

So the manager took several steps. In a series of one-on-one sessions, she took the time to listen to everyone in the group – what was frustrating them, how they rated their colleagues, whether they felt they had been ignored and so on. And then she directed the team in a way that brought it together; she encouraged people to speak more openly about their frustrations and also helped people raise constructive complaints during meetings. In short, her empathy allowed her to understand her team's emotional make-up. The result was not just heightened collaboration among members but also added business, as the team was called on for help by a wider range of internal clients.

Outstanding coaches and mentors get inside the heads of the people they are helping. They sense how to give effective feedback. They know when to push for better performance and when to hold back. In the way they motivate their teammates and demonstrate truest empathy in action.

Leaders with empathy do more than sympathize with people around them: they use their knowledge to improve their companies in subtle but important ways.

Social Skill

Definition – the ability to find common ground and build rapport with proficiency in managing relationships and building relationships.

Hallmark – effectiveness in leading change, persuasiveness, expertise in building and leading teams.

The first three components of emotional intelligence are self-management skills. The last two, empathy and social skill, underscore a person's ability to manage relationships with others. As a component of emotional intelligence, social skill is not as simple as it sounds. It's not just a matter of friendliness. Social skill, rather, is friendliness with a purpose: moving people in the direction you desire, whether that's agreement on a new outreach strategy or enthusiasm about a new service.

Socially skilled people tend to have a wide circle of acquaintances, and they have a knack for finding common ground with people of all kinds – a knack for building rapport. That doesn't mean they socialize continually; it means they work according to the assumption that nothing important gets done alone. Such people have a network in place when the time for action comes.

Social skill is the culmination of the other dimensions of emotional intelligence. People tend to be very effective at managing relationships when they can understand and control their own emotions and can empathize with the feelings of others. Even motivation contributes to social skill. Remember that people who are driven to achieve tend to be optimistic, even in the face of setbacks or failure. When people are upbeat, their *glow* is cast upon conversations and other social encounters. They are popular, and for good reason.

Because it is the outcome of the other dimensions of emotional intelligence, social skill is recognizable on the job in many ways that will by now sound familiar. Socially skilled people, for instance, are adept at managing teams

– that's their empathy at work. Likewise, they are expert persuaders – a manifestation of self-awareness, self-regulation and empathy combined. Good persuaders know when to make an emotional plea and when an appeal to reason will work better. And motivation, when publicly visible, makes such people excellent collaborators; their passion for the work spreads to others and they are driven to find solutions.

But sometimes, social skill shows itself in ways the other emotional intelligence components do not. For instance, socially skilled people may, at times, appear not to be working while at work. They seem to be fooling around – chatting in the hallways with colleagues or joking around with people who are not even connected to their 'real' jobs.

Socially skilled people, however, don't think it makes sense to arbitrarily limit the scope of their relationships. They build bonds widely because they know that in these fluid times, they may need help someday from people they are just getting to know today.

A leader who can't express his empathy may as well not have it at all. A leader's motivation will be useless if he cannot communicate his passion to the organisation. So, social skills allow leaders to put their emotional intelligence to work.

It was once thought that the components of emotional intelligence were *nice to have* in all leaders. But now we know that, for the sake of performance, these are ingredients that leaders *need to have*.

It is fortunate that emotional intelligence can be learned. The process is not easy. It takes time and above all, commitment. But the benefits that come from having a well-developed emotional intelligence, both for the individual and for the organisation, make it worth the effort.

II. Communication Skills

A. Interpersonal Communication

Think of how often you communicate with people during the day. You write emails, make calls, send messages, facilitate meetings, participate in conference calls, create reports or presentations, discuss with your colleagues... the list goes on.

Needless to mention, communicating clearly and effectively can boost productivity.

This is why the 7 C's of Communication are helpful. These provide a checklist for making sure that your meetings, emails, conference calls, reports and presentations are well constructed and clear so that your audience gets your message.

The 7 C's of communication are:

1. Clear
2. Concise
3. Concrete
4. Correct
5. Coherent
6. Complete
7. Courteous

1. Clear

When writing or speaking to someone, be clear about your goal or message. What is your purpose of communicating with this person? If you're not sure, then how do you think your audience will be!

To be clear, try to minimize the number of ideas in each sentence. Make sure that it's easy for your reader to understand.

People shouldn't *read between the lines* and make assumptions on their own to understand what you're trying to say.

Bad Example

Hi Vivek,

I wanted to write you a quick note about Shyam, who's working in your department. He's a great asset, and I'd like to talk to you more about him when you have time.

Regards

Vinay

What is this email about? Well, we're not sure. First, if there are multiple *Shyams* in Vivek's department, he won't know who's the one Vinay is talking about.

Next, what is Shyam doing, specifically, that's so great? We don't know that either. It's so vague, that Vivek will definitely have to write back for more information.

Last, what is the purpose of this email? Does Vinay simply want to have an idle chat about Shyam or is there some more specific goal here? There's no sense of purpose to this message, so it's a bit confusing.

Good Example

Hi Vivek,

I wanted to write you a quick note about Shyam Sharma, who's working in your department. In recent weeks, he's helped the IT department through several pressing deadlines on his own time.

We've got a new project and his knowledge and skills would prove invaluable. Could we please have his help with this work?

I'd appreciate speaking with you about this. When is it best to call you to discuss this further?

Regards

Vinay

This message is much clearer because the reader has all the information he needs to take action.

2. Concise

When you're concise in communication, you stick to the point and keep it brief. Your audience doesn't want to read six sentences when you could communicate your message in three. Ask yourself:

- Are there any adjectives or filler words that you can delete? You can often eliminate words like *for instance, you see, definitely, kind of, literally, basically*, or *I mean.*
- Are there any extra or unnecessary sentences?
- Have you repeated the point several times, in different ways?

Bad Example

Hi Manoj,

I wanted to touch base with you about the email marketing campaign we kind of sketched out last Thursday. I really think that our target market is definitely going to want to see the company's philanthropic efforts. I think that could make a big impact, and it would stay in their minds longer than a sales pitch.

For instance, if we talk about the company's efforts to become sustainable, as well as the charity work we're doing in local schools, then the people that we want to attract are going to remember our message longer. The impact will just be greater.

What do you think?

Jassi

This email is too long! There's repetition, and there's plenty of "filler" taking up space.

Good Example

Hi Manoj,

I wanted to quickly discuss the email marketing campaign that we analysed last Thursday. Our target market will want to know about the company's philanthropic efforts, especially our goals to become sustainable and help local schools.

This would make a far greater impact and it would stay in their minds longer than a traditional sales pitch.

What do you think?

Jassi

3. Concrete

When your message is concrete, your audience has a clear picture of what you're telling them. There are details (*but not too many*) and vivid facts but there's laser-like focus. Your message is solid.

Bad Example

Consider this advertising copy:

The Lunchbox Wizard will save you time every day.

A statement like this probably won't sell many of these products since there is no passion, no vivid detail, nothing that creates emotion and nothing that tells people in the audience why they should care. This message isn't concrete enough to make a difference.

Good Example

How much time do you spend every day packing your kids' lunches? No more! Just take a complete Lunchbox Wizard from your refrigerator each day to give your kids a healthy lunch and have more time to play or read with them!

This copy is better because there are vivid images. The audience can picture spending quality time with their kids. And mentioning that the product is stored in the refrigerator explains how the product is also practical. The message has come alive through these details.

4. Correct

When your communication is correct, your audience will be able to understand it. And correct communication is also error-free communication. Make sure your message is correct by asking yourself the following questions:

- Do the technical terms you use fit your audience's level of education or knowledge?
- Have you checked your writing for any grammatical errors? (Remember, spell checkers won't catch everything).
- Are all names and titles spelled correctly?

Bad Example

Hi Dinesh,

Thanks so much for meeting me at lunch today! I enjoyed our conservation, and I'm looking forward to moving ahead on our project. I'm sure that the two-weak deadline won't be an issue.

Thanks again, and I'll speak to you soon!

Best,

Jagmohan

If you read that example fast, then you might not have caught any errors. But on closer inspection, you'll find two. Can you see them?

The first error is that the writer had accidentally typed *conservation* instead of *conversation.* This common error can happen when you're typing too fast. The other error is using *weak* instead of *week*.

Again, spell checkers won't catch word errors like this, which is why it's so important to proofread everything!

5. Coherent

When your communication is coherent, it's logical. All points are connected and relevant to the main topic. The tone and flow of the text is also consistent. Let us understand this concept with the help of examples.

Bad Example

Tanvi,

I wanted to write you a quick note about the report you finished last week. I gave it to Michelle to proof, and she wanted to make sure you knew about the department meeting we're having this Friday. We'll be creating an outline for the new employee handbook.

Thanks,

Pradeep

As you can see, this email doesn't communicate its point very well. Where is Michelle's feedback on Traci's report? She started to mention it, but then she changed the topic to Friday's meeting.

Good Example

Hi Tanvi,

I wanted to write you a quick note about the report you finished last week. I gave it to Michelle to proof, and she let me know that there are a few changes that you'll need to make. She'll email you her detailed comments later this afternoon.

Thanks,

Pradeep

Notice that in this example, Michelle does not mention about Friday's meeting. This is because the meeting reminder should be an entirely separate email. This way, Traci can delete the report feedback email after she makes her changes, but save the email about the meeting as her reminder to attend. Remember, each email has only one main topic.

6. Complete

In a complete message, the audience has everything they need to be informed and, if applicable, take action.

- Does your message include a *call to action*, so that your audience clearly knows what you want them to do?
- Have you included all relevant information – contact names, dates, times, locations and so on?

Bad Example

Hi everyone,

I just wanted to send you all a reminder about the meeting we're having tomorrow!

See you then,

Krishna

This message is not complete. What meeting? When is it? Where? Chris has left his team without the necessary information.

Good Example

Hi everyone,

I just wanted to remind you about tomorrow's meeting on the new telecommuting policies. The meeting will be at 10 AM in the second-floorl conference room. Please let me know if you can't attend.

See you then,

Krishna

7. Courteous

Courteous communication is friendly, open and honest. There are no hidden insults or passive-aggressive tones. You keep your reader's view-point in mind, and you're empathetic to their needs.

Bad Example

Gopal,

I wanted to let you know that I don't appreciate how your team always monopolizes the discussion at our weekly meetings. I have a lot of projects, and I really need time to get my team's progress discussed as well. So far, thanks to your department, I haven't been able to do that. Can you make sure they make time for me and my team next week?

Thanks,

Raja

Well, that's hardly courteous! Messages like this can potentially start office-wide fights. And it does nothing but create bad feelings, which can lower productivity and morale of the team. A little bit of courtesy, even in hard situations, can go a long way.

Good Example

Hi Gopal,

I wanted to write you a quick note to ask a favor. During our weekly meetings, your team does an excellent job of highlighting their progress. But this uses some of the time available for my team to highlight theirs. I'd really appreciate it if you could give my team a little extra time each week to fully cover their progress reports.

Thanks so much, and please let me know if there's anything I can do for you!

Best,

Raja

What a difference! This email is courteous, friendly and has little chance of spreading bad feelings around the office.

B. Negotiation Skills

Let me explain three most important aspects of clear communication during any negotiation:

1. *Identify the intent of your communication*

When you are starting a conversation, firstly think about the intention of the discussion and the desired results you want to achieve.

When you speak with highly paid executives or high achievers, you will realise that they first understand the intent of the things they do or engage with. Why? Because they understand that having absolute clarity of the intent helps them stay focused and thereby achieve their desired outcomes.

So, to become an effective communicator, it is important to identify the intent of the communication and what the micro or specific objective is, that we are trying to achieve.

2. *Simplify the complex situations*

Many people try to communicate in a complex way, to show that they are brilliant communicators, and they know more than others. But what they don't realise is this... It is important to simplify complex problems if you want to become a brilliant and effective communicator. Anybody can make things complex, but your expertise stands out when you have the ability to simplify complex issues and break them down into small actionable chunks for the other people to understand well.

3. *Show the other person how they can get what they want*

If you want to achieve a win-win outcome from any communication or conversation, it is important for you to identify what the other person wants and then show them how they can achieve their desired outcome.

Once they can see that they can achieve what they want, you will then get what you want to. Let me explain this further.

You can't convince anyone to do something that they don't want to do. Agree? And the best way for them to agree on what you want, is by understanding what they want.

And when you become aware of what they want, you help them see how they can get what they want and eventually you will get what you want! It sounds simple, but what is simple to do is also simple not to do.

Now, here are a few tips you may consider to help create a win-win outcome during communication with other people.

- Be clear on the exact outcome you are seeking. It's important to know what you are ready to negotiate and what you won't negotiate.
- Being clear on whether it is more important to get a tangible outcome or maintain relationship. Listen intently to what they are saying.
- Ask many questions to check whether you are on the same page. You can do this but repeating the statement back to them in the form of a question.
- Observe the person's body language to see when they show signs of comfort or discomfort with certain questions or statements.
- To find out whether they are agreeing with you or not observe whether their arms and legs are crossed, if they

are leaning forward to backward and if they are calm or twitching.

- Find out the other parties motivation by asking open questions, listening intently and paraphrasing to check their understanding.

C. Persuasion

Persuasion is not just convincing and selling but learning and negotiating. It is not about trying to convince someone to agree with you. It's about getting a shared understanding and agreement. From there, you work together to reach a mutually beneficial outcome.

Leaders need to be good persuaders. They need to accomplish objectives through people. If they use persuasion effectively, they will lead their teammates to want to reach a shared solution.

Likewise, in any situation where you need to persuade someone to work with you or you want to promote your idea, if you pester them and advertise excessively, you'll only create resentment. Establishing mutual understanding is what leads to an agreement; one that is negotiated not forced.

4 Classical *Do*'s of persuasion:

- Establish Credibility
- Find Common Ground
- Produce Vivid Evidence
- Creating Emotional Connection

Establish Credibility

Not everyone can be persuasive in all contexts. A professor at a high-profile medical school has the potential to persuade people to participate in a clinical study, for example. That same professor will be much less persuasive when talking about the design of the medical college building. This type of credibility is based on expertise. When you are perceived as knowledgeable in, and experienced with, a particular subject, you are more persuasive.

The other basis for building credibility is through relationships. When you have built a reputation for taking a genuine interest in the well-being of your team and peers, your proposals and ideas are infused with that trust as well.

Find Common Ground

The next necessary element is making sure your position appeals to the audience. Even the most charismatic doctor will find it hard to recruit many participants for a study testing the effects of long-term radiation.

Establishing common ground is the closest you will get to "selling" your idea. There has to be an upside to your position so you need to determine what the benefits are. One of the most effective ways to do this is to analyse what has appealed to your audience in the past.

- Figure out what your audience is interested in.
- Meet with them and open up a dialogue about the issue at hand.
- Listen to their ideas and concerns.
- Run your ideas past people you trust first.

If you can't offer a clear benefit then you need to modify your position or proposal so that there is one. By talking with your audience first you can set up your position correctly from the start. This not just saves time, it also saves you from the likely embarrassment of presenting a poorly matched pitch.

Produce Vivid Evidence

Of course, you have to back up your position with evidence that what you are saying makes sense. A well-qualified physicist who wants to build a suit that will make people weightless has the credentials and an appealing proposition, but if his prototype is built on the premise that he can reverse gravity, he's going to struggle to find any takers.

Having evidence to support your position is critical. However, factual data and reams of spread-sheets and charts are not highly persuasive. What people respond to is vivid evidence that brings your concept or argument to life. For example, use metaphors to relate the concept to a shared reality, supplement data with examples and direct experiences, and think of analogies to make your ideas tangible.

This type of experiential proof is what causes shifts in people's perspectives and allows them to *see* the situation through the eyes of others who support what you are doing.

Create an Emotional Connection

Finally, no persuasive argument is complete unless you appeal to your audience's emotions. Some people think an emotional pitch has little credibility. When done correctly, however, it clearly establishes that you are plugged into your audience's needs and desires. So how do you appeal to emotions?

- Use your own emotions. This means showing emotions (enthusiasm and passion) when needed or suppressing them (anger and frustration).

- Sense the emotions of the audience – adjust your tone and intensity to fit your audience.

Emotions are primary factors in motivation and decision-making. As much as we'd like to be totally objective, it just doesn't happen. Appealing to emotions is not manipulative at all. It is a basic premise of persuasive communication and it helps facilitate a shared understanding of the issue and what is at stake.

Four classical *Don'ts* of Persuasion:

Each of the following is a common misconception about how to persuade, so it's important you are able to avoid them and recognize them when they are being used on you.

1. Don't Rely Only on a Great Argument

An argument is one component of persuasion. One or two strong arguments can be used as evidence that your idea is good, but you need to connect those arguments to emotion, and make them real by creating powerful images of what things would be like if people adopted your viewpoint.

A strong argument example: *Polls show that 82% of our hair salon demographic also purchases therapeutic massage treatments on a regular basis. If we were to offer in-house massages as an up-sell to our hair styling services, we would tap into this business stream and create a niche market all at once. I believe this is an idea that deserves financial and strategic analysis.*

A vivid and emotional argument example: *Our customers love to be pampered and they tell us this every day. I was talking to Shirley, who's one of our biggest fans, just yesterday about how good the scalp massages are. She says they are heavenly and suggests that Babita should be a masseuse. Thinking about this connection, I realised that our customers treat their hair appointments as an indulgent, luxurious experience. Why not offer them more indulgence? So I did some research and analysis and found out that 82% of people who match our demographic profile also purchase massages on a regular basis. Can't you just see our customers being treated to a massage before their appointment? Usually, when you leave a massage you look like a bedraggled mess. Here they come in, get pampered and leave looking more fabulous than they have in weeks.*

Do you see the difference in the impact? The argument is based on the same data but the presentation is what makes the persuasion factor.

2. Don't Make a Hard Sales Pitch

Everyone knows the hard-sell game. We are faced with it every time we go to make a major purchase like a car or home furnishings. What's the first thing we do in those situations? We get our back up and resist, argue or discount everything the salesperson says. We become opponents even before we know what we're fighting about.

Turn the situation around and make the presentation appealing by finding out what your audience thinks, values and needs. Then compose a position that isn't a target for attack, but one that has real merit and substance.

3. Don't Take an "All or Nothing" Stance

Persuasion isn't about forcing someone to surrender to your will. There are many points of compromise and collaboration. If you are inflexible, how do you expect to build trust? If you're not prepared to compromise, the other person has no reason to believe you have their interests in mind and no reason to be convinced.

4. Don't Believe You Have Only One Chance

Persuasion can take time to build. Many times you will not win people over with your first attempt. People need time to process and assimilate what you are saying with their current perspectives, beliefs and circumstances. A good persuader uses that to his or her advantage and layers his presentation using more and more of the "*Do*" elements each time.

D. Public Speaking

As a leader you need to address publically several times. Public speaking plays an important role in establishing your authority as a leader. Throughout the history great leaders have been identified by their phenomenal public speaking skills. Be it Abraham Lincoln, Martin Luther King, Steve Jobs or Narendra Modi. Moreover, if you speak a lot in public, language areas of brain become more developed. Here I am sharing some tips that can transform your public speaking skills thoroughly.

1. ***Speak around your passion.***

Passion is a positive intense feeling that you experience for something that is profoundly meaningful for you as an individual. Passion mobilizes a person's energy and enhances his commitment to achieve the goal.

People who are genuinely passionate about their topic make better speakers. It is a mistake to believe that you can influence others by speaking about a topic which is you don't love.

2. ***Master the art of storytelling.***

Abstracts are difficult for most people to process. Stories turn abstract concepts into tangible emotional and memorable ideas. *Stories are just a data with a soul.* Story stimulate and engage the human brain helping the speaker connect with the audience and making it much more likely that the audience will agree with the speaker's point of view. Storytelling is the ultimate tool of persuasion.

Brands as well as individuals who tell emotional and genuine stories connect with people in far deeper ways then do their competitors. Stories plant ideas and emotions into a listener's brain. During storytelling, speaker and listener develop a brain-to-brain coupling. The part of the solution to winning people over your argument is to tell more stories.

Three simple effective types of Stories-

a. Personal stories.

Take the audience on a journey of your life or a particular incident of your life. Make it descriptive and rich so that they imagine themselves with you at the time of event. Create some curiosity and mystery while narrating the story. The more personal is the story the better it becomes. No technique is 100% guaranteed but personal stories come close.

We often listen these types of stories in reality shows, where a contestant talks about ups and downs of his life and we get emotionally connected to that person.

b. Stories about other people.

Personal stories are about you but there can also the stories about other people to whom the audience can empathize. I personally use and recommend this style because not every time can we find the situation suitable to give our own examples. It is better if you take the example of an iconic figure while narrating this type of story.

c. Stories about brands success.

In the battlefield of ideas, marketers have a secret weapon – a well told story. Effective brand storytelling paints pictures of people, events, places, and experiences that connects audiences to the values a brand stands for.

3. ***Have a conversation.***

Practice relentlessly and internalize your content so that you can deliver the speech or presentation as comfortably as having a conversation with a close friend.

Authencity does not come naturally it comes with relentless practice.

Three steps of outstanding presentation –

a. Planning

Plan the structure and content of the presentation. Take help from your friends and colleagues, if needed.

b. Feedback

Practice in front of people, record it and watch it back. Ask friends and colleague to watch your presentation and to give open and honest feedback. Pay careful attention to the pace of your speech.

c. Rehearsal

Practice so many times so that you could deliver the speech or presentation without reading it. It makes people believe that you are an authority in the subject about which you are talking.

4. ***Say it in the way so people listen.***

The four elements of verbal delivery are: rate, volume, pitch and pauses.

Rate: Speed at which you speak.

Volume: Loudness or softness.

Pitch: High or low inflections.

Pauses: Short pauses to punch key words.

When you read printed text, it would be natural to use a highlighter to emphasize an important word or phrase. The verbal equivalent of a highlighter is to raise or lower the volume of your voice, change the speed at which you deliver the words, and/or set aside the key word or phrase with a pause before or after voicing it.

Ideal pace of public speaking is 150-160 words per minutes for audio books but in a personal presentation, it is 190-200 words per minute. For high energy motivational speakers, it goes up to 240 words per minute.

A great presentation is interesting and entertaining. Entertainers use their voices, facial expression, gesture and bodies to make is feel emotional.

5. ***Body language.***

If you don't believe what you are saying, your movements will be awkward and not natural. People are making judgments about you based largely on the way you walk, talk and look. So *talk, walk and look like a leader.*

Use gestures. Don't be afraid to use your hands in the first place. The simplest fix for a stiff presentation is to pull your hands out of your pockets and use them. Don't keep your hands bound when you present. They want to be free. Your gestures should be natural. If you try to imitate someone else,. Avoid canned gestures. Don't think about what gestures to use. Your story will guide them. Use gestures at key moments. Save your most expansive gestures for key moments in the presentation. Reinforce your key messages with purposeful gestures as long as it feels genuine to your personality and style.

Keep your gestures within the power sphere. Picture your power sphere as a circle that runs from the top of your eyes, out to the tips of your outstretched hands, down to your belly button, and back up to your eyes again. Try to keep your gestures (and eye gaze) in this zone. Hands that hang below your navel lack energy and "confidence." Using complex gestures above the waist will give the audience a sense of confidence about you as a leader, help you communicate your thoughts more effortlessly, and enhance your overall presence.

Tree easy fixes for common body language problems:

a. Fidgeting, tapping and jingling – observe yourself and write down all mannerisms that serve no purpose.
b. Standing rigidly in place – Movement is not only acceptable, it is welcome.
c. Hands in pockets – have an open posture.

6. ***Lighten up.***

Nowadays, sense of humor has become a highly prized personality character. Humorous people are seen as friendly, extroverted, considerate, interesting, intelligent, perceptive and emotionally stable. If you combined humor and novelty, you can deliver a marvelous presentation. Don't take your topic too seriously. Give your audience something to smile about.

How we present and how we deliver in presentations should be carefully crafted and considered.

a) Anecdotes, observations and personal stories that made you smile.

b) Analogies and metaphor that can bring smile to the listener.

c) Quote somebody else who said something funny.

d) Incorporate a humorous photograph or video clip to lighten up the mood.

Some additional tips:

- Be authentic, open and transparent. If you try to be something you are not, you will fail to gain the trust of your audience.
- You'll never make a lasting mark on impression on people unless you leave your own mark. Your goal should not be to deliver a presentation; it should be to inspire your audience.

End the speech or presentation on a high note: it may be an emotional story, a video, a demonstration or a personal anecdote.

CHAPTER FIVE

SELF MASTERY

How would you lead others if you are not able to do it yourself? Bring change in yourself which is recognizable and something that people want to make. You are a leader if people want to learn something from your life. Whether it's Mahatma Gandhi, Ratan Tata, Steve Jobs, Elon Musk or Narendra Modi, they are greatest leaders because people want to learn many things from them.

I personally observed in life that all life changes with a shift in mindset first of all. Then a process is to be followed, after which comes the expected outcome or change. So it all starts from changing your mindset. Swami Vivekanand rightly pointed out that mindset is the primary thing, everything else comes later on. Getting a profound mindset is the first step towards achieving anything in life. If you have not made up your mind to do anything, you just can't do it.

Attitude is something very important. We should always take care about things that might be difficult or easy, but our way of response definitely illustrates whether we are a good leader or not. So here are three things that not only help us gain personal mastery, but also help us become an impactful leader.

Mind your language

I'm not saying this to demean you or to scold you but minding your language is really important no matter where we are or whom we are talking to. Our language has an important impact on us. For example, if you always talk about in a positive way, then you feel positive and you will also have the guts to do something better for the society. But if you always talk to yourself in derogatory ways and just keep talking about the negative things, then obviously accomplishment of great things becomes really hard for you.

Till now I have discussed about mindset and ideas. Now let us focus on the implementation part.

Dream Hour

There are certain rituals which, if added to your daily routine, can really change your life for good. There are certain things I personally follow in my life like affirmations, visualisation, daily workout, meditation, journaling, book reading, goal writing and a daily spiritual process.

You should devote at least one hour deep work, which I call *my dream hour*. These can be anything that you think will settle well in your daily routine. I'm confident that these things will definitely transform you into a new being. My personal suggestion will be to slot this dream hour sometime during the morning when there is least distraction.

1% better every day

> “*“Success is a few simple disciplines, practiced every day; while failure is simply a few errors in judgment, repeated every day.”-Jim Rohn*”

The following article is an excerpt from *Atomic Habits* by James Clear, which I would recommend to everyone who wants to get transformation in life in a long term.

The fate of British Cycling changed one day in 2003.

The organisation, which was the governing body for professional cycling in Great Britain, had recently hired Dave Brailsford as its new performance director. At the time, professional cyclists in Great Britain had endured nearly one hundred years of mediocrity. Since 1908, British riders had won just a single gold medal at the Olympic Games, and they had fared even worse in cycling's biggest race, the Tour de France. In 110 years, no British cyclist had ever won the event.

In fact, the performance of British riders had been so underwhelming that one of the top bike manufacturers in Europe refused to sell bikes to the team because they were afraid that it would hurt sales if other professionals saw the Brits using their gear.

Brailsford had been hired to put British Cycling on a new trajectory. What made him different from previous coaches was his relentless commitment to a strategy that he referred to as "the aggregation of marginal gains," which was the philosophy of searching for a tiny margin of improvement in everything you do. Brailsford said, "The whole principle came from the idea that if you broke down everything you could think of that goes into riding a bike, and then improve it by 1%, you will get a significant increase when you put them all together."

Brailsford and his coaches began by making small adjustments you might expect from a professional cycling team. They redesigned the bike seats to make them more comfortable and rubbed alcohol on the tires for a better grip. They asked riders to wear electrically heated over-shorts to maintain ideal muscle temperature while riding and used biofeedback sensors to monitor how each athlete responded to a particular workout. The team tested various fabrics in a wind tunnel and had their outdoor riders switch to indoor racing suits, which proved to be lighter and more aerodynamic.

But they didn't stop there. Brailsford and his team continued to find 1 percent improvements in overlooked and unexpected areas. They tested different types of massage gels to see which one led to the fastest muscle recovery. They hired a surgeon to teach each rider the best way to wash their hands to reduce the chances of catching a cold. They determined the type of pillow and mattress that led to the best night's sleep for each rider. They even painted the inside of the team truck white, which helped them spot little bits of dust that would normally slip by unnoticed but could degrade the performance of the finely tuned bikes.

As these and hundreds of other small improvements accumulated, the results came faster than anyone could have imagined.

Just five years after Brailsford took over; the British Cycling team dominated the road and track cycling events at the 2008 Olympic Games in Beijing, where they won an astounding 60 percent of the gold medals available. Four years later, when the Olympic Games came to London, the Brits raised the bar as they set nine Olympic records and seven world records.

That same year, Bradley Wiggins became the first British cyclist to win the Tour de France. The next year, his teammate Chris Froome won the race, and he would go on to win again in 2015, 2016, and 2017, giving the British team five Tour de France victories in six years.

During the ten-year span from 2007 to 2017, British cyclists won 178 world championships and 66 Olympic or Paralympic gold medals and captured 5 Tour de France victories in what is widely regarded as the most successful run in cycling history.

How does this happen? How does a team of previously ordinary athletes transform into world champions with tiny changes that, at first glance, would seem to make a modest difference at best? Why do small improvements accumulate into such remarkable results, and how can you replicate this approach in your own life?

It is so easy to overestimate the importance of one defining moment and underestimate the value of making small improvements on a daily basis. Too often, we convince ourselves that massive success requires massive action. Whether it is losing weight, building a business, writing a book, winning a championship, or achieving any other goal, we put pressure on ourselves to make some earth-shattering improvement that everyone will talk about.

Meanwhile, improving by 1 percent isn't particularly notable – sometimes it isn't even noticeable – but it can be far more meaningful, especially in the long run. The difference a tiny improvement can make over time is astounding. Here's how the math works out: if you can get 1% better each day for one year, you'll end up 37 times better by the time you're done. Conversely, if you get 1% worse each day for one year, you'll decline nearly down to zero. What starts as a small win or a minor setback accumulates into something much more.

1% better every day $1.01^{365} = 37.78$

1% worse every day $0.99^{365} = 0.03$

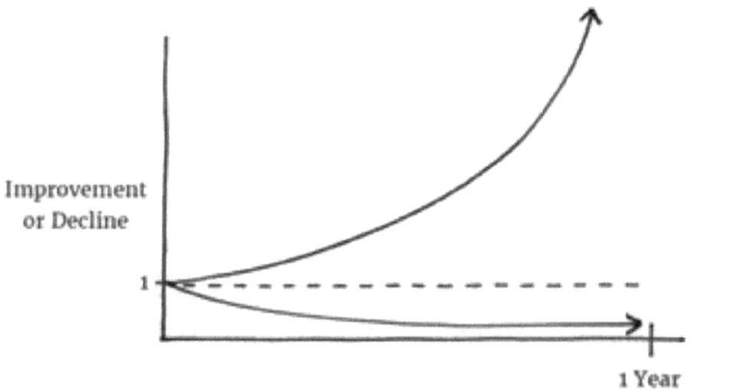

Compound effect of small gains

Habits are the compound interest of self-improvement. In the beginning, there is basically no difference between making a choice that is 1% better or 1% worse. In other words, it won't impact you very much today. But as time goes on, these small improvements or declines compound and you suddenly find a very big gap between people who make slightly better decisions on a daily basis and those who don't. This is why small choices don't make much of a difference at the time, but add up over the long-term.

7 Days Transformation Challenge

Starting today, you have to learn how to control your life and not let life control you.

Starting today, you have to decide that you'll not be a puppet to the circumstances but make the circumstances favourable for you.

Starting today, you will not wait for opportunities to come your way!

Now, are you ready for my 7-Day Transformation Challenge?

I want you to build your daily routine which consists of 5 simple, yet effective things. Start your day with *affirmations, visualizations, exercise, reading a self-help book* at least for ten minutes and *writing your day's goals down.*

Stick to this routine for at least seven consecutive days to see the change in the way you walk and the way you talk. It will transform your mindset and ultimately your life. The key here is *discipline.*

If you miss one ritual or miss all for a day, you will have to start from day one!

7 Fundamentals of Self Mastery

If you're still wondering about the 7 Days' Challenge, here's more to elaborate and guide you on how to go about it. This can be the set of activities of your daily Personal Leadership hour.

1. ***Learning***. Read from books that will inspire you, strengthen your character, and remind you of the examples of the greatest leaders of our world. Also, listen to audio

books on subjects ranging from business excellence, team building and innovation to wellness, relationships and personal motivation.

2. ***Affirmations***. One of the single best ways to rescript limiting beliefs and failure programs within your mind is through the consistent repetition of positive statements about the leader you want to become and the achievements you commit to create. For example, reciting the affirmation "Today I am focused, excellent, and stunningly passionate in all I do" a number of times at the beginning of your day will create the mindset of a champion and a winning emotional state for you.

3.***Visualisation***. The mind works through pictures. Every great accomplishment - from the largest statue (the Statue of Unity) in Gujarat to the most stunning inventions and discoveries of Indian geniuses like Aryabhatt, Charak, Sushrut and Bhaskaracharya began with a series of pictures set in the imagination of their creators. All outer achievements begin within the mind. All progress is nothing more than invisible creativity made visible. So during your Personal Leadership Hour, make time to close your eyes and - like any good elite athlete does - envision yourself realizing your goals, playing at your best, and fully awakening your inner leader.

4. ***Journaling***. Writing in a journal is a remarkably strong way to become a clearer thinker, to build massive amounts of self awareness, and to record your intended outcomes. During your hour of personal development, note your insights, feel ings, hopes and dreams. Also process through any frustrations you might be experiencing and go deep into your fears. The fears you embrace are the fears you'll release. Get to know yourself and reconnect with all the talent within you that's just waiting to be unleashed. Your

journal is also a place to express gratitude for all you have and to celebrate your journey through life. Your life is a gift. And so it's worth recording.

5. ***Goal Setting.*** Setting and then reconnecting with your goals on a regular basis is a powerful success discipline. Your goals will create a fantastic amount of focus in your career and within your life. Goals generate hope and positive energy. And when you experience adversity, clearly articulated goals offer you a North Star to guide you out of the rough seas into calmer waters. Goals also ensure that you live life deliberately and productively versus reactively and accidentally.

6.***Exercise.*** Doing something physical each day boosts brain function, fuels far higher energy levels, helps you manage stress more effectively and keeps you in the game longer.

7.***Nutrition.*** What you eat determines how well you'll perform. Leadership is influenced by your diet. By eating like a winner, your energy will remain at peak and your moods will stay positive.

Epilogue

It's not about you and me! We are here only for a limited time, but the society or our nation is forever. All our actions should sprout from the fact that you intend giving back to the society and you are contributing to the well-being of others. Needless to mention, the society consists of all kinds of people. Few people are ultra-rich. They can afford to buy airplanes and even islands. On the other hand, there are people who are struggling even for bread and butter.

If we keep earning and making money, and not paying back to the society, what will happen to our assets or factory or property if there is chaos? Our attention should also be invested for the long-term well-being of the society. *And that is real leadership for me!*

As there is karma of an individual, there is also a collective karma which needs to be taken care of. Whether it is knowingly or unknowingly, we are all responsible for the wrong things happening around us. There are many unprecedented problems our society has been facing lately. Women safety, pollution, global warming, terrorism, soil extinction and what not!

And what do we do to overcome these problems? We believe that a saviour or a superhero will come and he will end up all these global issues. At best, most people consider it their birth-right to curse the elected governments in such cases.

Well, we don't need any of these people really. We just need a leader to inspire us. People are waiting only for the initiation of things and the one who initiates the things, one who is proactive is called a leader!

Can we commit to give at least one hour for the society in a day? If that is not possible, then merely an hour in a week? If even that is not possible, then at least an hour in a month for some good cause? Is it really too much?

Here, I would also love to share my thoughts about *National character* and *Personal character*. If you look back at history, you will find that the land of India had always been full of brave and talented people in every part of the nation, but we still had to face successive invasions for over 900 years. Our culture was attacked, our temples were destroyed and all the wealth was plundered. As a country, if we look back and retrospect, we'll find that we could not realise our true potential. The reason is quite clear. Because barring some individual genius, largely, we lack in national character!

In 18th century, there was an Englishman named Clive who came to India because many people from the England were quite troubled by him.

So they wanted to get rid of him and decided to send him to India as a punishment.

And what he did in India? He just laid a strong foundation stone of the British Raj in India. Individually, though he was not a good person, he did great things for the British Empire because he had that national character I'm talking about.

If you're wondering how common men can contribute for the society, don't worry!

I have multiple options for you.

Volunteering

> *"Essentially, volunteering means to become willing, or in other words, to become an absolute yes to life. Most human beings are "yes" if it is convenient and "no" when it is not convenient; "yes" if it is yielding something, "no" if it's not yielding something for them. A volunteer means there's only one thing that he's dropped, which is a very significant thing. He has just dropped this one calculation, "What can I get?" If a human being drops this one calculation, suddenly he becomes a phenomenon. - Sadhhguru"*

Volunteering encourages individuals to work with other stakeholders and helps in building partnerships between those who may not normally work together. According to a survey, 92% of the respondents agree that volunteering is an effective way to improve leadership skills.

Volunteering enables individuals to get aware of them and their surroundings, empathize, and manage themselves and their relationships with others. All these skills directly or indirectly contribute to enhancing the individuals' emotional intelligence – a key to become an effective leader.

Giving back

The desire to give back is one of the greatest gifts written into the hearts of humanity. You don't have to look far to find someone who needs a friend, advice or shelter. The Creator provides each of us a generous bounty, which we can all share with the world through our time, money, love or help.

Giving and uplifting others is a way to pay it forward. It re-energizes you and makes you better. Giving also creates a culture of collaboration.

Supporting social causes

As a leader we are on a mission to make a positive impact on society and the best way to create this impacted by supporting some social causes.

Suppose a person is doing something good. Even if we have not initiated that, we must always see how we can support that person and bring about a positive change. What's important is not to get the credit, it's the internal satisfaction of doing something good that matters the most. Let's see how!

Can you imagine a man, aged 65, riding a lone motorcycle for about 30000 km, through 27 different countries and extreme climatic conditions?

Surprisingly, this bike rally was not for any personal gain. The only agenda was to make people aware about soil extinction and create a conscious planet. The man is none other than the visionary mystic Sadhguru Jaggi Vasudev!

It all started in the 1990s in rural Tamil Nadu. A group of people sat under the shade of a generous leafy tree, with eyes closed. A while ago, they had been sitting in the open, parched and sweating, feeling all the torrid effects of the southern Indian sun. Now, in protective green shade, with a cool breeze blowing, they realized the essence, and the benediction of the big tree. Sadhguru led them through an inner process, where they actually experienced the exchange of breath with the tree, breathing out carbon dioxide, which the tree inhaled, and breathing in oxygen that the tree exhaled - an experiential process where they clearly saw that one half of their breathing apparatus was hanging out there. These were the early days when

Sadhguru had just begun planting trees in what he called "the most difficult terrain – the minds of people." This first-hand experience of oneness with all life galvanized the first set of ardent volunteers who pioneered this movement to restore our planet.

What began with a few thousand volunteers in the 1990s in the form of *Vanashree*, an eco-drive aimed at greening the Velliangiri Hills, soon grew into *Project GreenHands*, a large state-wide campaign with millions of volunteers across Tamil Nadu in the first decade of 2000s. In 2017, when Sadhguru led the incredible Rally for Rivers, it snow-balled into the largest environmental movement on the planet supported by 162 million Indians, further leading to intense on-ground activity with the extremely hands-on, proof-of-concept project Cauvery Calling.

Now, the Save Soil movement includes billions of global citizens in an unprecedented movement to create a Conscious Planet and Save Soil. Sadhguru's mission to reach atleast 3.5-4 billion people on Earth has been the product of three decades of work and evolution.

One of the crucial aspects in the evolution of this movement has no doubt been the sheer number of people it has inspired. Estimates suggested that during the 100-day lone motorcycle journey, over 3.5 Billion people spoke about soil on social media platforms. However, equally important has been its growing levels of influence. From local communities, organizations, farmers, schools and state governments, to helping shape the National River Policy in India and now to working with some of the most environmentally-relevant international agencies, world leaders and governments – the movement has been making quantum leaps in the past three decades.

The phenomenal endeavor of the Save Soil movement was to bring citizens of the entire democratic world together to speak in one voice and affirm our commitment to the health and future of Earth. This has largely been a success!

When issues of ecology become electoral issues, when the people's support empowers governments to adopt long-term policy changes to safeguard soil, when businesses, organizations, individuals and governments make soil health a primary priority – that is when this sustained effort will find fruition.

The point here is that no matter who started the drive, we must own responsibility and support the cause as it concerns our future.

Try becoming an ideal citizen

Being a good citizen is very important. A good citizen is normally the type of person who works hard, helps others and respects the law. When reading newspapers or listening to the radio or watching TV, often, it is the activities of bad citizens that are publicized. Usually the crimes or bad incidents are reported because they make exciting news. However, we must remember that most people are very good citizens. Here are a few traits:

1. A good citizen is patriotic and vigilant.
2. He/she is active in the community.
3. Helps in protecting the national resources even if it is something as simple as switching off the fans when going out of the house or not throwing garbage on public places.

So that's it from my side for this time! Do not forget to write to me on how this book helped you. I want you to leave a review of this book on Amazon as it would really help me and mean the world to me. Counting my blessings is my real wealth as it keeps me motivated every day!

Love you. Have a Fantastic Life. See you in my workshop someday and in my next book!

9 798887 494388